Prais

MW00653458

"I love this book! It's as simple as that! Jenny McGill has penned a guidebook for growing in Jesus and following after Him. Its brilliance is its epistolary form. Each wise and warm letter to the reader epitomizes the gospel, which is never about information only. It is always about relationship. As a young Christian, this is the exact book I needed."

Leslie Leyland Fields, Award-winning author of *Crossing the Waters: Following Jesus through the Storms, the Seas, the Fish and the Doubt*

"Looking for a clear, easy-to-use guide to the basics of Christian living? And/or seeing a trusted resource as you mentor the next generation of Christians? Search no more. Jenny McGill's book, Walk with Me, is the perfect companion. Her solid understanding of the faith, presented in easy-to-understand language and filled with quotes and anecdotes, helps fellow pilgrims explore a wide range of topics on the road to maturity. Highly recommended."

Sandi Glahn, PhD, Associate Professor, Dallas Theological Seminary; author of the *Coffee Cup Bible Study* Series

"If you would like to be discipled and become a discipler, Jenny McGill has provided a clear, comprehensible, and transferable guide in Walk with Me. It is readable and practical. She reflects, with clarity and even humor, what the process looks like, what a disciple needs to know, and how a true follower can live increasingly like Jesus."

Judy Douglass, Writer, Speaker, Encourager, Advocate; Director, Women's Resources at Cru

"*Walk with Me* is a helpful introduction to the Christian faith that avoids stodgy, step-driven methods. Written in a warm, relatable style, this book covers key discipleship topics through brief letters that offer practical advice to Christian women."

> **Jonathan Dodson,** Lead pastor of City Life Church and Founder of Gospel-Centered Discipleship.com; author of several books including *Here in Spirit: Knowing the Spirit Who Creates, Sustains, and Transforms Everything*

"Finally, a discipleship resource that I can recommend for all generations. Jenny McGill explains heavy concepts for the everyday woman—taking the lofty and making it understandable. Each letter provides beautifully expressed, practical, and inspirational content for a discipler and a disciple to share on their journey together. Questions follow each letter that will lead to organic conversations required for true transformation. Walk with Me is a fabulous resource to enrich your discipleship journeys!"

> **Sue G. Edwards,** DMin, Associate Professor of Educational Ministries and Leadership, Dallas Theological Seminary; author of the *Discover Together* Bible Study Series (discovertogetherseries.com)

"For years I have looked for a comprehensive resource to help women who desire to take others through a discipleship process. Searching for something—that included not only the "what" of our beliefs, but that also touched on the "why" and the "how" of living the Christian life—always left me wanting. Until now. Jenny McGill has put together a book that I wish I had written. While the range of topics is lengthy enough to make a seminarian's heart beat fast, the format is simple enough for anyone to pick up and use. These letters evidence Jenny's thorough knowledge of discipleship, allowing any reader the privilege of great teaching, while the questions at the end of each letter encourage great discussion between those who are reading it together. This is every disciple-maker's dream resource."

> **Mitzi Arellano,** Pastor to Women, Fellowship Bible Church Dallas, TX

"I once heard John Perkins describe discipleship as 'teaching people to be Christian,' and that is exactly what Jenny McGill has done. Throughout this beautiful, encouraging, thought-provoking book, Jenny helps draw believers, both those who are new to faith and those who have walked with Christ for decades, into a closer relationship with Jesus. Written as a "big sister in the faith" to a younger sister, Jenny gives careful, biblical answers to many deep questions and covers every aspect of what it means to be a Christian in today's world. I highly recommend this book."

Shelly Wildman, Ministry Leader, College Church, Wheaton, IL; author of *First Ask Why: Raising Kids to Love God through Intentional Discipleship*

"As someone who has been mentoring women for over twenty years, I wholeheartedly appreciate new tools for biblical education and deepening together. Jenny's book is a timely resource in a culture fraught with automatic gratification and countless 'shiny things.' Discipleship can easily coast downhill into a glorified coffee date where the conversation ends on Hollywood or Netflix recommendations. Jenny's letters begin with a reminder of our identity in Christ and serve to lay a theological foundation in a tangible way, ending creatively to internalize the material. This book will help you fall deeper in love with Jesus as you walk beside others in spiritual pursuit."

Jen Bell, Ministry Leader and Pastor's Wife, The Well Community Church, Fresno, CA

"With a frank and candid view into her own life, Jenny writes with a relaxed, unintimidating approach. Her discipleship lessons are appetizingly digestible. She is spot on; I wish I had had this book in college. It is a true discipleship pearl for today and for future generations."

Sonya Dix, JD, First Lady, Pilgrim Baptist Church, Fort Wayne, IN

"With a warm, clear, and engaging style, Dr. Jenny McGill draws the reader to the profound life of discipleship to Jesus. In her hands, descriptions of the essential truths of God are filled with the wonder of soaking in God's goodness while reorienting the will and self to the daily saving work of God. Intended as a guide for those who are discipling others and as a roadmap for those longing to be discipled, this book of letters is well worth a slow and thoughtful meditation and conversation for those longing to grow in intimate relationship with our Lord."

Lisa Igram, Associate Dean of Spiritual Development, Biola University

"We were never meant to multiply buildings of mega-churches; rather, we were meant to multiply people as Christ-followers. This was Jesus's master plan. As Dr. McGill notes, few who claim faith in Jesus today have been discipled, let alone intentionally disciple others. *Walk with Me* is a theologically sound and practical, yet profound, tool for discipleship. The faith of both disciple and discipler will grow roots and bear fruit upon use of this resource. May more Christ-followers go, make, baptize, and teach disciples as a result of this work."

Karla D. Zazueta, Ministry Leader, Hispanic Ministries, Stonebriar Community Church, Dallas, TX; architect-turned-author of *Discipleship for Hispanic Introverts*

"When I was in my twenties, I attended a church with a women's mentoring program. The woman in charge told me, 'It may be two years before I have a mentor for you. I'm sorry, but I have many more younger women than older women interested in the program. Everyone wants to be mentored, but they feel challenged to be able to mentor.' Jenny has provided an indispensable tool by which many women can feel equipped to mentor. She has bridged the gap many feel between their own inadequacies and their desire to help others with this helpful guide. If you are someone who cannot find a mentor, Jenny is your virtual mentor through this book. Jenny won't let you be sold short on the process."

Lisa Ackland Carriere, Ministry Content Writer, Bible League International

"Jenny McGill's Walk with Me will encourage and provide direction for your spiritual journey. As a discipleship resource, Jenny offers a series of personal letters to women seeking to grow deep roots of faith. As a disciple of Jesus, as well as a discipler of women, I find Jenny's heartfelt letters filled with practical topics and thought-provoking application questions. Her engaging style combined with biblically anchored teaching will empower your discipleship journey and add a new resource to effectively disciple others."

Jan C. Thompson, EFCA Great Lakes District Coordinator of Pastors' Wives; retreat speaker and author of *Rooted Woman of Valor*

Walk

with

Me

Learning to Love & Follow Jesus

Jenny McGill

Walk with Me
Learning to Love & Follow Jesus

© *Jenny McGill*
All rights reserved.

GCD Books
Austin, TX

GCD Books is a ministry of Gospel-Centered Discipleship. Our purpose is to produce resources that make, mature, and multiply disciples of Jesus.

For more resources from Gospel-Centered Discipleship, visit us at GCDiscipleship.com/Books and follow us on Twitter @GCDiscipleship.

Front cover design: Laura Schembre of Copper Street Design (copperstreetdesign.com)
Back cover & interior design: Benjamin Vrbicek (benjaminvrbicek.com)

ISBN 13: 978-0692160145
ISBN 10: 0692160140

To Annie.
We are beautiful and broken and being made new.
Don't let anyone sell you short.

For Sharon, Ana, Maritsa, and the MVEC girls.

For any old soul who thirsts for more
than they have found on this earth.

Acknowledgments

Kathy, Diane, and Janis: You have spent years shaping women, and I thank you for choosing to invest in me. This book is, in part, a tribute to you. Irene, Toni, and Jessica, thank you for your encouragement during the completion of this project. Gratitude is due to the Redbud Writers Guild, whose collective wisdom has been so helpful at every stage of writing, publishing, and marketing, particularly to Shelly Wildman. I thank Indiana Wesleyan University and the Lilly Endowment Foundation for supporting this project through a faculty grant that I received. I especially thank Dr. Herbert Jarrell for editing the initial manuscript, all those at GCD involved in bringing this book to press, and Andrea Himmelsehr for her final editing of this project.

Also, I married a writer. This has inevitably shaped me. Thanks to my husband, I pretty much have my own private tutor living in the house. I may have penned the letters, but his love for discipleship also spills onto these pages from our many talks together about the subject.

Lastly, I thank you, my reader. For those who want to live to love God but have not had someone to walk with them on the Way (Acts 9:2; 11:26), I wrote this for you. Annie, one of the girls I discipled, was my inspiration, but you, dear reader, were the reason.

Contents

Part Three: Habits of a Christian

Part Four: Reading the Bible as a Christian

Special Topics

Read This First

I write these letters to you for one reason—life! With the love I have for all the people I have met over the years, I write in the hopes that you will find life and happiness and joy and laughter and freedom. Those things do not come just any old way (Proverbs 8:35–36; 16:25). You must decide if what I describe is the path you wish to walk.[1]

Many claim faith in Jesus. Fewer are discipled.

Discipleship is a fancy word meaning how you mature in Christ, how Christ is formed in you—in your thoughts, your actions, your life. Discipleship is not church attendance or Bible study. Some folks who have gone to church their entire lives have never been discipled. Take me. I went to church for almost twenty years before I was actually discipled.

Discipleship usually happens in pairs of women or men (wherein one of whom having already been discipled guides another). Discipleship is a walking together in the way of Christ, learning to die, learning how to leave who you were, and learning who you now are. Learning to follow Jesus, becoming his disciple, means walking alongside someone further in the Christian faith for a significant period. It is personal. It is challenging. Jesus walked with his disciples for three years. This is no six-week curriculum. My husband once remarked to me:

People have no issue when they hear someone told, "Here, spend the next four years of your life learning how to kick this ball," but when it comes to discipleship—learning how to live like a Christian—churches offer a six week curriculum, as if that could cut it. Isn't that curious?

Discipleship is often done one-on-one because it allows the two to go much deeper than in a group. Smaller groups of three to four folks can work also. Jesus had his twelve, his inner circle of three on whom he focused, and his special one, John (who, interestingly, was the only one left standing at the cross when Jesus died). So whether meeting one-on-one or in a small, intimate group, it must be consistent, comprehensive, personal, and penetrating. Discipleship is opening yourself up so completely to another person to let her look into your life in the secret places with a level of spiritual honesty and vulnerability that you have not given to anyone else. It's not coaching. It's not counseling. It's not BFFing. Your personalities may not mesh for a long-term friendship, but for the time of discipleship, you respect this woman enough to learn from her.

How do babies learn to walk? Search "babies walking" to check out a few YouTube videos and observe the process.[2] What made the difference for these babies? They had someone ahead of them, giving them direction and encouragement. It took trust. It took practice. It involved laughter. There were some mistakes, successes, falls and pick-me-ups. There were distractions and interruptions. That's a lot like learning to walk in Christ.

Whether or not you have been discipled before, think back to when you first learned about God. Who was involved in that process? In the same way, as we learn to follow Jesus, we cannot learn to walk in Christ by ourselves. What do you see happening between these two?

For me, this is a picture of discipleship. Discipleship is walking together for a period of time, discussing life's challenges and God's answers together.

What about me? I grew up in church and learned a lot of Bible stories. At age fourteen, I was distinctly called out by the risen Savior to follow him in a personal experience. For anyone who has met the living Christ, you know what I mean. Whether the call occurs in an explosive rescue or a quiet encounter, it is real. I would not suggest you seek a certain type of experience. Seek Christ. He invites you in a most compelling way to reach you personally and uniquely. If you have not experienced an actual time where you sensed God in Christ calling you . . . ever . . . perhaps you might ask for it. Ask to meet the living God personally

(Revelation 3:20). We are told when we are God's (Romans 8:16).

It was not until my sophomore year at university that I was discipled. I knew a lot about God by then, but it was another gal living in the dorms who literally walked with me—for two years—through what following Christ looks like on a daily basis. Over the years, I have had several women continue to disciple me along the way of my faith. Kathy first grounded me in my faith. Diane pulled me out of a deep pit I had dug. Janis helped me to start living the new life I had in deeper ways.

Discipleship has at least five parts, in my opinion. These are in no particular order, and the Bible is studied throughout the process to inform each of these:

#1 Beliefs of a Christian
#2 Living like a Christian
#3 Habits of a Christian
#4 Learning God's Word (the Bible)
#5 Special topics specific to your life's journey

My mum and dad faithfully taught me #2 and #3. My Sunday school teachers taught me #1 and #3, sort of, with gaps. Diane and Janis each helped me with #5. Kathy was the one who taught me all five, over a concentrated two-year period.

I wrote this book to start you on a discipleship journey with someone, covering the five areas listed above. I thought writing letters might make it easier to understand while also making it more personal. There is a lot to learn and even more to apply, and the second part is much harder. Take it slowly.

This book is arranged into four parts. Part One discusses what a Christian believes. Part Two describes what a Christian looks like (or should look like). Rather than explaining a list of dos and don'ts, I describe virtues as ways of being, ways one lives as a Christian. These will guide you then in what to do or not do in a given situation. Part Three offers the habits of a Christian—the exercises that shape your spiritual muscle tone, so to speak, and strengthen you in your Christian experience. Part Four summarizes the Bible, breaking it down into parts to give you the big picture of Scripture and how it all masterfully weaves together. Lastly, I cover some special topics of common interest that did not fit into the previous chapters. At the end of each letter, you will find a set of questions that you should answer with your discipler and/or those you disciple.

Directions

I suggest that you read one letter at the start of your week, taking the rest of the week to chew on the topic. Take your time, ask good questions, search the Scriptures. Take longer than a week if you like. If you follow this schedule, roughly, these letters will take about one year to finish.

These letters form a discipleship manual of sorts, covering the basics to start your faith journey. Ideally, read these letters with someone, hopefully the person who is discipling you or whom you are discipling. The verses listed throughout each letter are embedded hints for the questions at the end. Work through the questions together, using these verses. The open-ended, general questions are meant for you to explore ideas. You may learn as much about yourself from your answers as the questions. The

Christian faith is not just about you and Jesus; it is to be shared, so asking these questions in community, or at least with someone else, is best. I have tried to cover the main subjects, but please understand that this is but a broad overview as a beginning point. There is much, much more to discover!

Grab a Bible. The New International Version (NIV) may be a good option. I list the relevant verses as I write. Be sure to stop and read each one. It is far better that you read God's Word to you on these matters than my faulty gibberish alone. If this is the first time you have studied the Bible, you should know that when I write John 3:16, for example, it means that you would look in the book labeled "John," look for the big number, 3, in the text that is the chapter of the book, and locate the tiny superscript number, 16, that stands for the verse.

Disclaimers

I have tried to represent broadly and fairly the multiple traditions within the Christian church (Orthodox, Protestant, and Catholic) while also staying true to my personal convictions and theological training. That is a tricky balance, and some may question my representation of their position.

Inevitably, in such a short book, I will not be able to cover or discuss in detail all the facets of the Christian life. Think of this as a handbook to get you started as a disciple.

First Things First

You certainly do not have to be a Christian to read this book. It may just be that you want to learn more about

what Christians believe. If as you read along, you discover
that Jesus might be the answer to life, here is something
like what you might consider saying to God:

*Dear God, It's simple. I need you. I believe that Jesus
is the Son of God, died on the cross, and rose again
to save me from evil and death and myself. I have
done wrong, but I believe that you have forgiven me.
I give you my life. I choose to turn from my way to
follow you, to turn from what does not please you.
Fill me with your Spirit. Show me how to live. I am
yours now. Amen.[3]*

Part One:

Beliefs of a Christian

1

Getting Started

Dear Reader,

Since you may be new or old to this Christian thing, don't feel badly if you stumble over the big words. It's quite a lot to take in! When I was seven years old, my parents gave me a plaque with the Bible verse, 1 Timothy 4:12, which they thought particularly suited me. That plaque has served me well, and will you:

> *Don't let anyone look down on you*
> *because you are young,*
> *but set an example for the believers*
> *in speech, in life, in love, in faith, and in purity.*

Paul was referring to Timothy's age here, but, in another sense, "young" can refer to someone young in their faith. Many have not grown up in church and are learning what it means to be a Christian as an adult. Don't mind anyone older in the faith who might stomp on your eager enthusiasm in your newfound faith. It's a new, old, old story. Christians believe certain things about God that are different from other religions, and it actually matters. Relating to God is not something you just make up as you go along. God sets the terms. We can agree or disagree with them. We may even try to change the terms, but in the end, God will set us straight.

I can do no better to summarize the basic beliefs of our Christian faith than the creeds that the global church over the centuries has passed down to us. Christians face different challenges in each culture in which they apply God's Word, and the church creeds stand as a summary of the main beliefs. I have included two: the Nicene Creed and the Apostles' Creed.

Apostles' Creed[4]

I believe in God, the Father Almighty, Creator of heaven and earth; and in Jesus Christ, his only Son our Lord, who was conceived by the Holy Spirit, born of the virgin Mary, suffered under Pontius Pilate, was crucified, died, and was buried. He descended into hell; the third day he rose again from the dead; He ascended into heaven, and sits at the right hand of God, the Father Almighty; from thence he shall come to judge the living and the dead. I believe in the Holy Spirit, the holy catholic[5] Church, the communion of saints, the forgiveness of sins, the resurrection of the body and life everlasting. Amen.

Nicene Creed[6]

We believe in one God, the Father Almighty, Maker of heaven and earth, and of all things visible and invisible; and in one Lord Jesus Christ, the only-begotten Son of God, begotten of the Father before all worlds; God of God, Light of Light, very God of very God; begotten, not made, being of one substance with the Father, by whom all things were made, who, for us for our salvation, came down from heaven, and was incarnate by the Holy Spirit of the virgin Mary, and was made man, and was crucified also for us under Pontius Pilate. He suffered and was buried, and the third day he rose again, according to the Scriptures, and ascended into heaven, and sits on the right hand of the Father, and he shall come again, with glory, to judge the quick and the dead, whose kingdom shall have no end. And we believe in the Holy Spirit, the Lord and Giver of life, who proceeds from the Father [and the Son]; [7] who with the Father and the Son together is worshipped and glorified, who spoke by the prophets. And we believe in one holy catholic and apostolic Church. We acknowledge one baptism for the remission of sins, and we look for the resurrection of the dead, and the life of the world to come. Amen.

A third creed, the Athanasian Creed, also explains our faith. I do not include it here, but you can find it online easily. These beliefs are what church leaders debated for centuries to determine together what was God's message to us as recorded in the Bible so that we wouldn't misunderstand. These creeds don't cover everything we should believe as Christians; but they showcase what was much debated at that time to preserve the unchanging message of the gospel through the centuries that is for us now. We are the direct recipients of the councils who sought clarity to best represent the unchanging truth of the unchanging One (Malachi 3:6).

Follow the ancient paths (Jeremiah 6:16),

What Do You Believe?

1. What parts of these creeds do you find difficult to understand or to believe?

2. What phrases in these creeds do you readily believe?

3. Does holding to certain beliefs, as a Christian, matter? Why or why not?

Notes:

2

Under New Management

Dear Daughter of God,

When you became a Christian, you accepted the gospel message: that Christ's death and resurrection on the cross saves you from being forever separated from God and that you are reborn into a new life in Christ to pursue the kingdom of God. You know those guys who stand on the corner with a sign plate on the front and back sides of their body announcing "Tacos $2" or "Car Wash to the right"? It's like you now wear a sign over you indicating that you are "Under New Management."

Not everyone understands immediately what being under new management means, mind you. I understood the first part of this as a child and vaguely the second half, which God was faithful to explain more fully when I was old enough to understand. And God does bring his children along but not on their own. That's why a new Christian desperately needs to be in a good church and be discipled by someone more firmly set in the faith for a significant length of time. Many have said they believed and have not moved beyond that—for years. They remain stunted, and worse, may be misled to believe that they are Christians when, in fact, they are not.[8]

Upon becoming a Christian, a beautiful journey with God begins that has its ups and downs and turnarounds, but God carries you in your faith. At age nine, I understood I was a sinner and accepted what Jesus had done for me. When I was fourteen, during a pastor's sermon, I sensed that I should be following Jesus in every area of my life. Seriously. I was suddenly convicted that Jesus was asking me to choose him over anything else in life. Jesus will literally compel you to a moment of decision. It doesn't have to be fancy or bold or loud, but within your spirit, you will know.

Those moments continue as he walks with you through life. You'll get to those places where you would rather walk your own way, and the Spirit of God nudges you that this is not the path for you. And we all know those times we've ignored God. We can pinpoint those as well as the moments we did follow God. I have marked mine as milestones in walking with God: at ages 9 and 14 as I mentioned, and at ages 18, 21, 25 and 29 to name a few most significant.

My point is that you have given up however or whatever you used to live by (at least in theory) and have placed yourself voluntarily under new management. You will falter, object, and thrash violently at times against this new will of yours (which is to say, of Christ's) because your old will—your old sense of things—is still hanging on for dear life. It does not want to die. All the verses on dying to yourself, cutting off the old ways, will begin to make more and more sense. The power resisting God (evil) does not want to let you go. The truth is that you have already been saved.

So, that's great news, but a battle will be fought for the whole of your life. I kid you not. But you knew that already because you have felt it.

Stay close to God's Spirit,

Jenny

What Do You Believe?

1. What Do You Believe God wants for you?

2. Since becoming a Christian, what area(s) are under more of the Spirit's control?

3. How can you tell what God wants you to do? Hint: My letters under the section "God Speaks" should help.

Notes:

3

God is Creator

Dear Daughter of Eve,

Nature has a remarkable voice. Let God speak to you through it. If you gaze into the expanse of the galaxy and are caught up in wonder, if you look at the elaborate veins of a tiny flower petal and are struck with its intricacy, then you have experienced the marvel God intended (Romans 1:20). Most of the world's inhabitants have believed that a supernatural power formed the world. They are not necessarily primitive in their thinking. Scientific discoveries have not solved the riddle of what or who started it all. For example, the big bang theory does not explain *how* or *why* those first particles appeared.

I like how my friend describes her conviction. After graduating from high school, she and I wrote long letters to each other during university and discussed our differing beliefs. She was majoring in philosophy, and I loved reading her thoughts. She is an extremely gifted and intelligent woman. In our writing, she shared that she believes in a SGGOAM—Something Greater Going On Around Me. Her sense of awe in something beyond us is what many have realized: there is more to what we see. Both—believing in a designer or believing that chance started it all—require faith. God, in great mercy, continues to bless and sustain those who acknowledge God as well as those who do not (Matthew 5:44–45).

Debates rage regarding how God started the world (whether six literal days, over longer periods of time, or by theistic evolution). Some believe in an old earth without believing that primates were our ancestors. Some Christians also readily hold to the existence of microevolution while not macroevolution. This is too brief a letter for that discussion here; right now, I want to focus on the *Who*. We believe, as Christians, that God is Creator, forming the world and giving life to billions, from spermatozoa to humanity, through the centuries. We believe this because God has given us his word that this is how it happened (Genesis 1–2; Revelation 21–22).

May you realize God's deep love for you in bringing you into existence,

What Do You Believe?

1.   Why did God start this world in the first place? This is
     a huge question for you to work through with the
     woman discipling you but an important one. What
     does Scripture tell us?

2.   Why do you think God created you specifically?

3.   With God as Creator, what is your part to play in this
     world? Hint: Genesis 1:28; Colossians 3:23.

Notes:

4

God is Three in One

Dear Beauty,

One thing about you is how relational God made you. The ability to relate and your desire for relationship did not start with you. Relating is deeply like God. God is relational. So when we try to comprehend God the Trinity, perhaps how God relates within God is a helpful way of thinking. There's no easy way to explain the triune God, and I know this is the one thing you struggle the most to understand. Join the club!

I would give you an example of God the Trinity if I could, but nothing that has been created resembles how God interacts within God. No analogy that I have found— not an egg, a pie, apple, sun, shamrock, water, triangle, etc.—compares. What ends up happening (and the problem) with examples are that the three persons of God are either reduced to three parts, instead of three wholes in One, or simply represent one person. YouTube has a three-minute video on the Trinity that might help and make you chuckle.[9] God is revealed to us as the triune One, as one God and three persons of the Father, the Son, and the Holy Spirit. No illustration—that is, no man-made representation of what this could mean—explains it. God as Trinity is a fantastic mystery beyond our comprehension, and what

God would we serve if we could understand God's indescribable depth (Romans 11:33–36)?

The belief that God is the triune One distinguishes us from other religions that do claim only one God exists, such as Mormonism, Judaism, and Islam. None of these hold to our Trinitarian belief that God is One in three persons. Each person of the Trinity possesses a unique identity, a personhood, and an identity defined in relation to the other two. While it does reflect three persons in one being, the Trinity is not composed of three individuals. I know, it's complicated!

Does it matter? How does God relate to you from day to day? Think about each person of the one God for a moment. If we did not have God the Father, how would we have life and breath (Acts 17:24–28)? God the Father knows all and guides all there is to control (Matthew 6:8; Mark 13:32). If Jesus was not God, we would not be forgiven of our sins. We still would be weighed with shame, trapped in Satan's taunting. We would have no Savior and divine Attorney (1 John 2:1). If we did not have the physical manifestation of God in Jesus, how would we know who God is? If the Spirit was not God, how would we be empowered? With God's Spirit inside of me (1 Corinthians 3:16; 6:19), I have access to God and hinder it only by my lifestyle choices to walk away from God. As my husband says, the Spirit is our chaperone. Without the Spirit, I would not be drawn to God or convicted of sin (John 16:8). God the Spirit teaches me, encourages me, comforts me, inspires me to hope, guides me, reassures me, gifts me, empowers me, prays for me, directs me, nudges me (Acts 2:36–37). Those are gifts only God possesses. May you be overwhelmed with awe as you contemplate God. God the

Walk with Me

Father is our loving Dad. God the Son is our Liberator. God the Spirit is our Promise (Ephesians 1:13–14).

Praying for you, dear friend,

Jenny

24

What Do You Believe?

1. What is the role of each person of God in your life? Hint: Read each of the verses above.

2. What do we learn about life and God by the Trinitarian nature of God?

3. How would you describe the Trinity to someone else? (This one's for practice!)

Notes:

5

Five Things about Jesus Christ:
Jesus is God

Dear Sister in Christ,

Good morning. I'm wondering what you will face today as I write this letter. I care for you very much, and since you have chosen to give your life to Jesus, I want to clarify who he is. You will spend the rest of your life getting to know him, and five things about him are the most important. Let me explain.

Christians believe that Jesus is God. God is one God as Father, Son, and Spirit. But why must we believe that Jesus is God—besides the fact that God said it in the Bible (Philippians 2:5–6)? What difference does it make in our daily lives?

Well, for starters, we could not reach God on our own, not by any of our attempts. People have tried dozens of things through the centuries to satisfy their gods (pleas, gold, jewels, incense, sacrificing children, sexual displays). What have you tried? What do women offer to please today's world? Being thin, being sexy, being successful, bearing children, being a perfect wife and/or mother, doing it all? The most beautiful thing about God, I think, is that God in mercy and love stooped down to us. To us! In other words, we were powerless in and of ourselves to reach God. The construction of the tower of Babel is another example of our complete and utter useless attempts to find God on our own (Genesis 11:1–9). The very reason that you came to God was because you personally have discovered this truth for yourself. You gave up and asked God for help.

But why must Jesus be God? One reason Jesus must be God is for our salvation, so that we will not be dead forever. God is perfect, and his perfect love requires judgment of all injustice and wrong. We participated in that wrong which separates us from God forever. No amount of effort in our futile attempts to please God will change that. We are utterly desperate because we are stained by sin. God as Love did not want us to die and be separated forever. Instead of getting what we deserved, God in Jesus was judged on the cross for all the evil in the world. If Jesus had been merely a man, then he might have died to pay for his own sins, but no one else's. If Jesus is not God, then our guilt still hangs in the universe over us like a two-ton weight.

This brings me to another reason why it matters to us that Jesus is God. God as Jesus in human form grew up like us, suffered as we have (and much more), and identifies with our every human desire and need. God's ability to identify with us was because God lived out a human existence, of birth and death, and every scrap and sour note and sensation in between that life brings. The indescribable God understands us completely, and because God lived among us, *we* can know that God understands us (Hebrews 2:14–18).

Thirdly, we need Jesus to be God because we need constant intervention in our lives. God the Son, Jesus Christ, having taken our death sentence, now pleads for us to God the Father on a continual basis (Hebrews 7:25; 1 John 2:1). Who better to pray for us than God himself? Because he identifies with us completely, who better to represent our case to the God of the galaxy than God? As sinners standing guilty before a divine judge, we need a very good lawyer! We are comforted that God is not distant and unable to relate to us; rather, God has come near to us because Jesus is God (James 4:8).

One other side point. That Christians believe Jesus is actually both human and God distinguishes our beliefs from all other religions, namely, Mormonism, Islam, and Judaism. When you talk with your friends of other faiths, cut to the chase, and focus on this distinction. It will highlight your differing beliefs. For now, spend some time thinking about what I've written and *why* Jesus has to be God.

Because Jesus is God, you have everything you need (2 Peter 1:3–4),

Jenny

P.S.
You might enjoy Andrew Peterson's song, "All You'll Ever Need," on his album, *Resurrection Letters, Vol. 2.*

What Do You Believe?

1. What would we lose if Jesus had only been a human being?

2. What would we lose if Jesus was only God?

3. What area(s) of your life do you have trouble believing that God understands?

Notes:

Jesus is Human

Dear Rescued,

As you start your day, scurrying to juggle various tasks and people in your life, I want you to know that you are never alone. God is close and wants to be near you. Why? Because God loves you very much and understands what you're going through. How? In part because God in Jesus existed within human form to experience the daily tussles we get tangled in.

What is the big deal for Jesus to be human? Nobody debated it when he walked down the rough roads of Jerusalem. They debated then if he could be God (Luke 20:1-6; 22:66-71). Later, Christian leaders debated whether or not he was actually a man (google Arius and Athanasius). The church council in Nicea (in the year 325) decided together that God clearly revealed that Christ was a real dude, full flesh and blood, and noted it in the Nicene Creed.

So again, why does this matter? Firstly, we believe because this is who God described Christ to be (through the written record of Scripture, through the apostles, through the early church fathers). Christ "made himself nothing, taking the very nature of a servant, being made in human likeness. And being found in appearance as a man ..." (Philippians 2:7–8a). Reading that, we start from belief and reason then perhaps ask why. Theological books already explain quite well the necessity of Christ being both God and man as a central and irrevocable Christian belief.

It matters—not hypothetically, not theoretically, but practically for you—*why* Christ was human (Of course, even if it didn't matter practically to you, Christ's humanity would still be true). Christ being human means that he can be our substitute in life and death:

- The prophecy about the special Savior came true (Isaiah 7:14; 9:6–7; Micah 5:2). Would God be proven a liar if he promised something that he did not do?
- Christ, because he was a man, fulfilled the life required of us that our ancestor, Adam, failed to do, and Christ died physically to be judged for humanity's sin (1 Corinthians 15:21–22). This is how we are saved from our sins.
- Through Jesus, God has a way to identify with us. Would we want God to understand what we go through on a daily basis?

God, even before Christ lived on earth, identified with us. As the prophet Isaiah said, "And so he became their Savior. In all their distress he too was distressed, and the angel of his presence saved them. In his love and mercy he redeemed them; he lifted them up and carried them all the days of old" (Isaiah 63:8b, 9).

Christ felt human in every way, which means that he can represent us in the best possible way to our Father in heaven (Hebrews 2:17). If you wanted someone to represent you in court, who would you pick? Someone who could communicate your concerns most accurately? The world is a stage for the ultimate court case of the cosmos, and if God is human in Christ Jesus, we have reason to hope. So hold onto hope this week as you run your errands and pay your bills, as you deal with this co-worker and that relative, as you wait for that insurance claim to finally come through. For this we know: God is for us (Psalm 56:9).

Love,

Jenny

P.S.
Joan Osborne's song, "What if God were One of Us?" from her album, *Relish*, comes to mind. The lyrics are curious, relative to what I just wrote.

What Do You Believe?

1. What do you need help with in life right now?

2. What could God possibly do about it?

3. What needs have others expressed to you this week? How will you help them?

Notes:

Virgin Birth

Dear Daughter of Mary,

I wish I had known you when you were younger, as you searched for the good life and looked for where to start. I wouldn't have had all the answers, but I could have been your friend. No girl likes to be left out in the cold, alone and afraid. Mary, also young, unmarried, and pregnant, felt that fear before things were explained to her (Luke 1:26–38).

Mary, a teenager and blessed among women, would conceive and bear the only Son of God by God's Spirit. Jesus was born to a virgin, one of the most fantastic mysteries of all time. That's the third thing about Jesus that Christians believe.

Why God in all greatness would condescend to inhabit the womb of a woman—it's incredible. It's unbelievable. Well, almost. We believe, not because we grasp it, as if we possessed an unlimited source of knowledge, but because it is what God foretold (Isaiah 7:14; 9:6–7; Micah 5:2). If God said it and it didn't happen, if God predicted something that wasn't fulfilled *exactly*, then God wouldn't be God. And who believes in a God who makes mistakes? God only speaks truth, and he's never wrong about the future.

This was the way God chose to rescue us. How? Why? When?

God moved at a very specific point in history (Romans 5:6; Galatians 4:4). How the world counts years revolves around Christ's birth; human history turns on *this* event. Signs are everywhere—including how years are counted—for people to have a chance to believe in the one true God through the Son, Christ. It's amazing.

We are given a reason why this matters. God is the first author and wrote the greatest story in creating and rescuing the world, full of the elements of symbolism, foreshadowing, conflict, resolution, etc., typical of literature. God started history with Adam, who blew it when it came to obedience (Romans 5:12–19). God saved history with Christ, the Son of Man, who aced everything Adam didn't. See the parallel? God is intentional, and everything God does, whether we understand or not, makes sense. Christ would not have fulfilled his Son of Man role unless he was physically born from a woman. Also, Christ would not have fulfilled his Son of God, being fully God, unless he was miraculously conceived by God's Spirit, rather than a male. Mary's virgin birth brought forth both.

God loves you so much that God entered this world by way of a tender girl to rescue you. God, ironically, came to save us in the most vulnerable of positions, a baby. God was born by human blood, placenta, and pain into this cold, messy world to bleed for you.

Now go, live God's good life.

Loving the outlandish story of God and you,

Jenny

P.S.

As a side note, Mary is a remarkable lady who played a major role in the great story of God. But was Mary perfect or divine? Not being perfect or divine makes Mary unhelpful to receive prayers. Offered as a form of worship, prayers only are for God. God tells us that we have only one person who petitions for us, and it's not Mary. It is God through the Son and Spirit (Romans 8:26–27; Hebrews 7:25; 1 John 2:1). Jesus does respond to someone praising Mary, and it's curious what he says (Luke 11:27–28).

What Do You Believe?

1.   Why did God enter history this way?

2.   Why would God choose a humble girl like Mary?

3.   How are you similar and different from Mary?

Notes:

His Crucifixion

Dear Cherished,

I always love hearing a bit of good news. From trees budding with the freshness of spring to a project completed at work, I listen and look every day for good news. Look for a little good news in your day, like the unexpected success that comes your way, the kindness someone showed you, how you held your tongue when you could have spoken, the provisions God makes for you. By now, you've learned the greatest news in the whole world.

Ironically, the best news ever is the most graphic, violent, and bloody affair in history: the death of the Son of God. Christians believe that Christ's death was absolutely necessary. What kind of good God would take life if it wasn't? But why? Why did Jesus Christ have to be killed? Beside the fact that God told us what would happen (Isaiah 53:5–12; Mark 14:58; John 2:19), why does it matter that Christ physically died on those wooden beams so many years ago? What do you think?

That moment in time changed history and the possible screenplay, if you will, for our stories. God has always been serious about the wrongs we have done. Adam, as humanity's spokesman, first broke God's heart, and each of us has done the same thing since. How would the cycle stop? How would reparations be made? Do we think God will look the other way? Will God ignore the unfathomable wrongs committed through the centuries—of people destroying each other, of leaders demanding money from the vulnerable, of intentional ignorance, of the lies we tell? When we write down what we should have done and did not and what we have done that deserves judgment, we feel a little bit like a criminal. Not everyone believes that they are guilty, so they feel no need to be saved. But for those of us who admit we are (guilty), why are we saved by Christ's physical death?

Evil requires a blood payment.

Like it or not, wrongdoing, according to God, earns physical death (Romans 6:23). God presumably made the first animal sacrifice for the first couple who wronged him (Genesis 3:21), demonstrating for the Jewish people that their guilt required animal sacrifice. The most amazing grace is that God does not require our death for our sins (that would be justice); God died for us. God's ability to forgive our sins follows the judgment of them. If Christ was not killed physically, then our sins are on us to pay.

This is all well and good, but on a daily basis, what does Christ's death mean for you? It means that with each new morning that dawns, you can wake with hope. You can walk in joy and peace. It means that you can sleep with a clear conscience. It means that you can forgive yourself because God has (Psalm 51) and let go of the hurts that others have done to you, forgiving them (Matthew 18:21–22). It means that when you fail, you can honestly claim fault, address it, and move forward. With God's physical death through Christ, we are freed from the weight of shame, condemnation, and spiritual death. If God personally left heaven to pay for our sin, a death that should have been ours, to give us a second chance at life—and we refuse—what more can be done?

I love you, and try to imagine how much God loves you,

Jenny

What Do You Believe?

1. Did God have to die on the cross? Why?

2. What was accomplished by God's dying on the cross?

3. As Christians, God calls us to that same death daily. Read Galatians 2:20 and the verses surrounding it. What do you think about what these verses say?

Notes:

Jesus's Physical Resurrection and Return

Dear Treasure of God,

What superhero power would you possess if you could? You know that I could not write all of these letters without bringing up comics at least once! And for the record, Batman does not have any superpowers. Hah! But seriously, what superpowers are popularly chosen? Becoming invisible? Super strength? Acute hearing? Controlling minds? Flying? I haven't heard anybody mention this one: raising people from the dead.

Of course, we can't reduce God of the universe to a superhero, but to be a Christian is to believe that Jesus Christ literally rose from the dead. It was a recorded historical event with witnesses, but some still question whether it happened. Some of the Jews (those who did not believe that Christ was their Messiah) and the ruling Romans would have been *very* motivated to find Jesus's dead body to quell the rumors. Remember, most of Christ's followers at that time were common laborers and relatively poor. They would not have had the resources or training to concoct a conspiracy. Others have written about this at great length (see books by former atheist, Josh McDowell, and journalist, Lee Strobel). God declared it to us, but why was it necessary (1 Corinthians 15:1–8)?

Remember that weight in your heart that you can never measure up or please God? You know the shameful things we've done that we hide in dark places in the closets of our hearts? Christ's death alone was not enough to save us. His death paid for our sins, but what brings us to life after death? His resurrection! The resurrection signals for all time that God is satisfied. Justice has been served. The guilt that hangs over us can be lifted. Love wins for the one who understands what she actually deserves and accepts what Jesus had to do for them.

Because God the Spirit now lives in you (John 14:16–17, 26; Acts 5:32; Romans 5:5), your physical death will be temporary. Jesus's death and resurrection give you a new life, a rebirth, into God's family. Jesus himself has promised to return to this earth (called the "Second Coming" in Christianese) to conquer evil once and for all and collect you to bring you safely home (Mark 13:24–37; Luke 17:22–37; Acts 1:10–11; 1 Thessalonians 4:16–17; 2 Thessalonians 1:7–10; Revelation 1:7–8).

With love,

Jenny

P.S.
"Hallelujah, What a Savior" is a hymn that beautifully describes what Jesus has done for us. Find it online. It's one of my favorites!

What Do You Believe?

1. Since Jesus's resurrection is neither something we witnessed nor can prove now in a scientific way, how do you believe it happened? Why?

2. What did Jesus's resurrection bring? Hint: 1 Corinthians 15:2–18.

3. What does Jesus's resurrection bring to you each day?

Notes:

6

God Speaks

Dear Redeemed,

Do you like to talk? Do you prefer to hang back and speak only if necessary? Words can beautifully express love to others. Words, as you know, can burn your heart deeply, searing into your memory for decades. Think of that time when that person said something so misguided or hateful that it branded you. We are meant to feel deeply, and words can wonderfully draw those feelings out or shut us down. Words lend truth or lie, and sometimes it's hard to tell the difference.

Incredibly, God chose to bring the world into existence through spoken word (Genesis 1:3–26). God gave the word of Scripture to guide us, offered Jesus as the Word of God, and speaks to us through the Spirit. What a vulnerable way for God to pronounce his love for us. In determining God's voice, we must look at multiple sources from God to make sure we do not misinterpret God. Creation, the life of God in Jesus, the Holy Scriptures, and God as Spirit speak together in unity and agreement. Mistakes are easily made, so be cautious in what you claim is of God or from God. Others name prayer, the church, mature Christian individuals, and circumstances as useful in discerning God's voice and will. These are helpful and must align with the four (creation, Jesus, the Bible, the Spirit) that I will describe below. Read the first one on creation now since I merely introduce the section as a whole here.

Much love,

Jenny

God Speaks: *Creation*

Dear Reflection of God,

This morning while writing this, I heard the first mourning dove of spring cooing outside my balcony. How does it know to return? What prompts its cycles and instincts? I love to hike, and often vibrant and varied hues color my path with the hushed silence of beauty. Nature is our treasured gift.

Christians believe that God spoke creation into existence. Your mouth might drop when you read that. The biblical account conveys that the earth was created in six days. I believe these were six actual days; others debate the days as figurative. I think a dose of humility and accepting the mystery of the cosmos are key. What we do believe as Christians is that God created all of reality. It is God's good creation, and we should love and protect it. Read how thrilling God's earth is in these chapters: Job 38–39, Psalm 8, and Psalm 104.

Nature inspires and fascinates and can draw us to God (Romans 1:18–20). Several of my friends actually came to believe in God while walking in the woods. Their hearts were opened so that later, upon hearing the gospel, they accepted its message of salvation. Nature, to this day, is the way that they feel closest to God. It's beautiful. For those of us who live in urbanity or suburbia, we need to creatively find ways to be in nature, among God's creations. One of my friends, for example, built a grapevine in her backyard to better understand John 15. Some people garden, bird watch, or raise chickens; others hike, camp, or travel. While you live in the city, make sure you are intentional about watching nature. Find a state park, a mountain, a lake, a patch of quiet. Breathe in the fresh, cool, dewy air of an early morning, watch the elaborate spinning of a spider whose shiny web blocks your path, traverse a creek and see what you find, take in the brilliant hues of a sun saying goodnight . . .

Ask what God might be saying to us through nature,

Jenny

What Do You Believe?

1. What is God saying to us through nature?

2. Why did God create the world? Hint: Genesis 1:2, then look at 1:3–26.

3. In what new way can you begin caring for God's earth this week?

Notes:

God Speaks: *Jesus*

Dear Graced,

I've already written about Jesus in earlier letters. I need to draw out one more point about Him, and as you will find, discovering Jesus brings new thrills and more questions. As for how God speaks to us, one of the four main ways that God does is through the life of Jesus. Because Jesus is God, we get the closest anyone has come to understanding God by learning who Jesus was. Understanding God isn't an assignment we can finish promptly to check off a list. Like any relationship, it takes time, effort, and commitment to know God. Whatever we think God is saying to us in the twenty-first century will match what Christ said and the rest of what God has already said. God does not lie or change (Numbers 23:19; Malachi 3:6; Hebrews 6:18). God writes one grand story from Genesis to Revelation. Look for the links. Some passages are tricky to understand, so it's important to learn together in a community of faith and learn from others who have studied the Bible longer. Seeming contradictions may become clearer to us over time. I've already written about Jesus in a previous letter (see "Jesus is God"), but my point here is that Jesus is the mouth of God. What Jesus said and what he did is a window into who God is and how God thinks (John 1:9–

18; 14:6–11). Jesus said, "Whoever has seen me has seen God" (John 14:9).

May the God of hope fill you with all joy and peace as you trust in him, so that you may overflow with hope by the power of his Spirit (Romans 15:13),

Jenny

What Do You Believe?

1. In the Bible, is there anything in particular Jesus said that you have trouble believing?

2. What do you wish Jesus would have talked more about while he was here (wishing it had been included in Scripture)?

3. What is getting in the way of your hearing God this week?

Notes:

God Speaks: *The Bible*

Dear Precious,

You are such a good student. Whether or not you have a formal degree, you have chosen to read these letters and are far enough along in your reading now to prove me right, that indeed you are a great student. You want to grasp more of what God has said to us over the centuries. It will be worth it. I am so proud of you.

God chose to speak our present world into existence and come to earth in the form of a man, to speak through a book. The Bible claims to be God's words of truth (Psalm 19:7–8; 2 Timothy 3:16). God chose language to reveal meaning. Know that some of the scriptural manuscripts have errors in transcription (those who transcribed the words of Scripture made mistakes in transferring data). These corruptions are basically typos, and the words that were miscopied do not change or affect the original meaning of the text. In other words, the manuscripts have no errors in their *meaning*. This is hugely important. Dr. Daniel B. Wallace has written multiple books handling this (e.g. *Revisiting the Corruption of the New Testament*), and I recommend watching the excellent video of his recorded debate with Dr. Bart Ehrman, "Can We Trust the Texts of the New Testament?"[10] Surely, God could and did preserve the message intended for us.

New archaeological discoveries are found that help decipher previous texts, like the Qumran scrolls found in 1947, or the limestone block found in 1961 that mentions Pontius Pilate. That stone dates as first century, which means it existed during the time that Pontius actually lived. Previously, only the Bible had mentioned his name, and scholars doubted its veracity. This plaque and a few coins now corroborate the biblical evidence. Here's a photo I snapped during my time in Israel.

A replica of the Pilate Stone in Caesarea, Israel.

Individually, and even as a group, sometimes we can get a certain phrase or verse of the Bible wrong. Having the Old Testament helps us so much in interpreting the New Testament, and Jesus and his disciples show us how (see, for example, Matthew 5:33–48; Acts 10:34–43; Romans 3:4–20). Different Christians from various cultures over time give us a better and better picture of what God meant by the words we have in print. It's also so important to read the Bible as a whole and often, rather than focusing on the bits and pieces we like.

The books forming our Bible were vigorously vetted by previous church leaders as far back as the year 170 by Melito of Sardis, and the Christian church affirmed its completion by 397.[11] Christians agree with Jewish scholars on the number of books (39) included in the Old Testament. The fancy word is canonicity, meaning, these books form the canon, or catalog, of God's actual words to us. Dating, authorship, historical details, and other considerations helped our church fathers agree on which books were authentic. The Catholic Bible includes a few more books. For Protestants, those books do not demonstrate sufficient authenticity to be God's Word. Both groups, however, agree on the shorter list of 27 books in the New Testament and that no new books will be added. Since you know how hard it is for a group of people to agree on anything, this is impressive. Look at Congress, or a school group project, or your family deciding what to do on vacation.

The canon is closed, meaning, no new books will be added. Why? For one, it would be highly unlikely that a previously undiscovered, completely new manuscript would be found at this late date. Even if one was found, it would be very hard to verify by itself. New manuscripts of *existing* copies may be found, but think of how many copies we would need to find of a completely new book to verify its authenticity. Tens of thousands!

The point is, if you choose to believe that the Bible is God's word, so much factual, scientific evidence supports that decision. I list a few resources at the end of this book of letters. The Bible claims to be the words of God to give us hope (Psalm 19:7–8; Psalm 33:4; Romans 15:4; 2 Timothy 3:16; 2 Peter 1:20–21). Ultimately, believing that these are his very words is a decision of faith. We believe that God is real and that God delivered a message to us this way. Psalm 119 sensationally describes God's words to us, and this refers only to the Hebrew Scriptures written at that time!

> *103 How sweet are your words to my taste,*
>   *sweeter than honey to my mouth!*

> *105 Your word is a lamp for my feet*
>   *and a light on my path.*

> *114 You are my refuge and my shield;*
>   *I have put my hope in your word.*

> *128 Because I consider all your precepts right,*
>   *I hate every wrong path.*

> *160All your words are true;*
>   *all your righteous laws are [forever].*

God promises to shape your heart by his Word,

Jenny

What Do You Believe?

1. What questions do you have about the Bible in general?

2. Was there a time when a verse in the Bible "spoke" to you and touched you in a special way?

3. What are you looking for when you read the Bible?

Notes:

God Speaks: *The Holy Spirit*

Dear Child of God's breath,

When you want to get a message to someone, how do you normally do it? Perhaps you speak to them, or type an email, or write a letter. It's interesting to me that of all methods, God also chooses to use words.

God spoke the world into being. God spoke to Abraham, Hagar, Moses, and through loads of prophets, priests, kings, and peasants from approximately 4000 B.C – 1 B.C. Then, give or take a few years, God was born into human existence and spoke directly as a man, Jesus.[12] The Bible tells us that God the Father called from heaven and endorsed Jesus as God's Son with God's Spirit in the form of a dove alighting upon him. John records this as his personal experience and eyewitness account in John 1:32–34. There in Jesus's baptism is a beautiful encounter of the Trinity, God acting as One in three Persons. It's deep.

In a fascinating twist after Jesus was raised from the dead, God the Spirit enters those who have become Christians (Acts 2:4, 38). Jesus had already promised that God would send his Spirit (John 14:16–17). So how do we know if we have God's Spirit within us? Read Romans 8:22–30, Ephesians 2:22, and 1 John 2:20, 3:24. For anyone who accepts that they've blown it, that they can't get to God on their own, and believes that Jesus died to pay for what they actually deserve and that he rose from the dead to give them a new life in God, God's Spirit enters that person mysteriously and instantaneously. God then speaks to Christians through his Spirit in them. This is tricky, though. How do you know if what you are thinking or feeling is God speaking, a lack of sleep, our archenemy (the devil), or a bad taco? Very tricky, indeed.

A lot has been said in God's name that has not been God at all.

A whole lot.

Here's the deal. We should be very careful before claiming to speak for God. God the Spirit will not speak anything in contradiction to what God the Father has already said in Scripture or what God the Son said since they are One. God does not lie or deceive and does not create disorder or chaos (Psalm 89:34; 1 Corinthians 14:33). No one should add to what God has said (Revelation 22:18-19). What God the Spirit does do is reveal new perspectives of the same truths. God has been very clear about certain things and less so about others. We should maintain a similar emphasis. The big idea things like morality and ethics, God has made plain in Scripture and repeats in Jesus. To be sure, God's Spirit talks often to us about certain things—to correct our behavior, to draw us to God, to convict us of our guilt, to guide us, to console us, to intercede for us (Romans 8:26-27).

We must read Scripture as a whole, together, understanding how the Old and New Testaments connect. Some books, frankly, misinterpret or misrepresent God. Remember, Satan would love to see us hang, to trip us into misunderstanding what God said. He is the father of lies (John 8:44) and fooled our ancestral parents embarrassingly easily. See Genesis 3 where Satan disguised himself as a beautiful serpent to trick them.

Sometimes we may only feel sure it was God's Spirit or "a word from the Lord" in hindsight after much time and reflection has passed, and often, only as we have a better understanding of the Bible and who Jesus is through study, time, worship, and prayer in a community with other believers. I cannot stress that enough. If you are trying to figure out if God is saying something in particular to you through God's Spirit, do not decide that by yourself (1 John 4:1–6). Wisdom is found in many counselors (Proverbs 15:22). If God is speaking, God usually says it several times in different ways so that we will not miss it. If you do not have those multiple indications, pointing in the same direction, I would pause. As my Irish friend often says, quoting an unknown source, "Novelty in theology is not necessarily a virtue."

I know you've struggled with knowing what God has wanted you to do. You are earnest. Many of the decisions you will make daily are not a big deal. God has given us the Spirit so we can walk in freedom to make those kind of decisions without flipping out. But when it comes to questions of morality, ethics, and big life decisions, that's where we'd want to hear from God. After all, we are no longer our own; we belong to God.

Stay in step with the Spirit of God,

Jenny

What Do You Believe?

1. What questions do you have about God the Spirit?

2. Can God's Spirit leave you? Can you affect God's Spirit? Hint: Ephesians 4:29–5:3. Think through what the words "grieve" and "seal" mean.

3. How can you tell if it is God's Spirit speaking?

Notes:

God Speaks: *The Church*

Dear Friend,

Church. What comes to your mind when you think about that word?

God initially plucked one individual (Abraham) from a sea of people and started a tribe, a group known as the Jewish people (Genesis 11–25). Throughout the Old Testament, God prophesied a coming Savior who would save Abraham's descendants and the world (Romans 1:2–4). Most Jews do not believe Jesus was this Messiah, the promised one from God. Those who do are called Messianic Jews. Several explain how this transition took place with Jesus (Matthew 5:17; Acts 7:2–53; Ephesians 2:12–22; Hebrews 9:15–28). He is the Jewish Messiah because he fits all the prophecies foretold and perfectly fulfilled the law that God first gave to the Jewish people.

How in the world does this relate to you?

Well, you have the Jewish God and people to thank for your faith in their Messiah. You have been included in their salvation (Romans 1:5–7; Ephesians 2:11–13). The Jewish people remain a very special population to God, and he will fulfill all the promises he ever gave them as recorded in Scripture. How God has done that or will do that is debated.

Whereas God's presence hovered in the Jewish temple, once Jesus died, that changed—dramatically. Read Luke 23:44–46 and Hebrews 9:1–14. When the holy Jewish temple curtain that had previously shielded and protected people from God's holiness (and thus, his wrath over wrongdoing) *tore*, Jesus's death accomplished something that all the millions of animals sacrificed had never done. His death saved us and the world. The Messiah accepted the ultimate judgment of God on all evil, pain, and death everywhere in the universe at once. God's wrenching split the world wide open, literally, to overcome our separation from God (Matthew 27:50–54). God explained where his presence moved (John 14:16–17; Ephesians 2:19–22). Ever since the events recorded in Acts 1, God's presence, his Spirit, dwells in each of us who have believed in what God did on the cross. The temple in which God resides is now our bodies. Talk about a miracle!

Why the shift? Why would God change how he first set up things? We may not know completely, but I think part of the answer lies in God's plan to save the world. The Master Architect knows just what temple to build to accomplish his goal. People can move. If there's one thing God wants to create, it's access. Access to a very important message to save the world. In the Old Testament, God's Spirit spoke to people and entered a few folks temporarily. In the New Testament, after Jesus's time on earth, God the Spirit came and filled God's people (Acts 2). So when God's Spirit enters a new believer today, it's permanent. God's presence in that person then meets people wherever one goes.

The church. Jesus is the foundation of God's temple now built of people, the cornerstone. Each believer is connected to each other in this amazing design of God's presence around the world. Besides the word temple, Jesus refers to the church as one body, a familiar image to us. God speaks to the world through *us* (I know, a scary thought) and speaks to us through each other. That is why being a part of a local church is super important. Parts form a whole. Don't be a random, isolated part. Imagine a lone limb flailing about on its own trying to figure out God's will, as if it could live apart from its body. A sorry sight, indeed! You will hear from God in a different way through the church than just on your own. The church is a new tribe of people, a family spliced into the first group that God created to worship him, the Jewish people (Romans 11:11–12). I know this is heavy, dear. Hang in there!

Stay close to God's folks,

Jenny

What Do You Believe?

1. Think through the church experiences you have had. Are there moments you need to sort through, people you need to forgive?

2. If a child asked you, "What is a church?" how would you describe it?

3. How could you respond to someone who says they won't go to church because of all the hypocrites inside?

Notes:

7

Other Mysteries of the Christian Faith:
The Image of God

Dear Imagined by God,

No matter what you have heard through your life, you are beautiful beyond words. You are valuable. You are priceless. No one else can be or do what God wants to do through you in this world. Your self-worth comes from somewhere, from Someone. You are fundamentally distinct from members of the animal kingdom.

This relates to the Christian belief that humanity is made "in the image of God" (Genesis 1:26–27; 5:1–3; Romans 8:29; 1 Corinthians 11:7; 2 Corinthians 3:18; Ephesians 4:22–24; Colossians 3:9–10; James 3:9). What does *that* mean? You are more than your instinctual behavior, that is, you bring more to the table than an animal could. You are a complex, intricate, and complicated being who reflects something of who God is. Last time I checked, no one was really arguing that God is an animal.

Being made in the image of God is described in three ways. Some believe we image God in how we act, reproducing the restorative activity of God on earth. Others believe we image God in how we are related to God. The traditional view is that we image God in being a person, reflecting God in our very being.[13] The image of God may best be described as personhood, something a human is as a being, from which follows the capacity to relate and act. Thus, being in proper relation and function to God (and others) displays the image of God perfectly. Have you ever met a son or daughter who reminds you so much like one of their parents in the way they think, look, or act? This is kind of the same idea.

This religious belief grants the individual value of each person and of human dignity. This truth directs how we treat people every day—our co-workers, the store cashier, the person who nearly sideswipes us merging in traffic, our neighbors, our estranged relatives, those marginalized in mainstream society. We don't treat others with dignity to get something from it; we treat others with respect because they were made by God, no matter how they act toward us.

Remember who you are and whose you are. We love because God first loved us (1 John 4:9).

With love,

Jenny

What Do You Believe?

1. How valuable do you think you are to God?

2. What about Jesus would you like to mirror well?

3. Who among your family, friends, and co-workers could you treat better this week?

Notes:

Marriage

Dear Loved,

You may not have seen a great many marriages lived out. That's not how it was meant to be. I am sorry for the pain that you were caused by the adults in your life making bad decisions, sometimes repeatedly. It affects you. This does not mean that your marriage cannot be beautiful. Wait. Hope. Ask. Prepare. Live. Don't hold out marriage as the prize; your goal is to run toward God and his calling for your life.

I also want you to understand what marriage is. Oneness in difference. Marriage is mysterious. Stunning. Sacrificial. God describes marriage in Genesis 2:20–25 at the beginning and reiterates it in Ecclesiastes 9:9 and Malachi 2:14–15. Jesus reaffirms it in Matthew 19:4–6.

Almost from the beginning, those who claimed to follow God also followed some of the not-so-great practices they picked up from their neighbors (of different religions) like polygamy. When you consider that wealth, power, and status were tied to how many sons you had in the Ancient Near Eastern culture, taking multiple women to increase your odds of male births would almost make sense, if not for faith in God. Imagine how hard it would have been for the minority group of Jews struggling to survive to trust that God would provide for them without them having to resort to the common sexual practices of the day—about as hard as it is for us to trust God today.

Even Abraham and Sarah caved and regretted it (Genesis 17:4–6, 18; 21:9–11). Polygamy creates its own set of problems, but I'll explain that later. The point is that God designed marriage a certain way. When people stray from this, they get hurt (Genesis 4:19, 23–24; Deuteronomy 17:17; 1 Kings 11:1–8). God is merciful and slow to anger, so God lets us make our own choices (Exodus 34:6). But what God says is true is the only path to life and happiness. We fool ourselves to think that God will let us cut corners and that it would still work out (Galatians 6:7). Yes, God lets us live our own way, but see also Proverbs 14:12.

What is marriage? God defines marriage as between a man and a woman in a physical union of bodies and spiritual union of hearts to make one new whole. Your body doesn't know the difference between dating and being married, so when a couple become sexually intimate and later split up, it is heart-wrenching. Sex is a sign of intimacy that was intended to pair two people only after they first made the decision to commit themselves to each other for life in marriage.

Who you marry becomes your blood relative and family in a more profound way than your birth relatives. Marriage is the intertwining of two hearts and bodies, being one yet being different, being one yet with diverse opinions. Ask anyone who's ever been married. Difference creates friction and yet can create a complement that is one of God's finest achievements (Genesis 1:26–31; 2:20–25).

Marriage teaches us things we need to learn about God the Trinity. Marriage is about creation, about family, about safety, about growth, about change, but it is chiefly about sanctifying, growing the husband and wife in holiness (Ephesians 5:26). Marriage is the arena for sex—the enormous and wondrous stadium for the intimacy of two people, now one, to fill! Great sex doesn't work any other way. By having sex our way, we cheat ourselves on the greater thrill we might actually have by doing it according to the directions. I have many friends—who are single, divorced, widowed, or married to someone who cannot perform sexually—who are not sexually active and living full lives, so it is entirely possible and better to wait. Would God cheat us?

Put your joy in God and wait on the rest (Psalm 37:4). In the meantime, live! Enjoy where and who you are at this very moment. It's a gift from God.

Love and hugs,

Jenny

What Do You Believe?

1. Has God cheated you in the area of relationships? Has anyone else? How?

2. What characteristics would you want in a husband?

3. What do you think God had in mind to do when he created marriage for us?

Notes:

Baptism

Dear Prized,

If someone's been baptized as a baby, should they get baptized again? Why do some parents wait and have their children decide for themselves when they are baptized? If you have already been baptized, do you realize what was happening when you were?

Baptism is an outward symbol of an inward change, as my husband likes to say. It's a sign that you are a follower of Jesus Christ. Baptism pictures Jesus's story in his death, burial, and resurrection, and your joining his story in death (going down into the water), being buried (underwater), and being raised to new life in Christ (coming up from the water). You were dead under God's judgment, but because of what Jesus did, you were washed from sin and reborn, now with God the Spirit living inside of you.

Without too much of a historical lesson, I will share that the Jewish people practiced baptism, but for a different purpose. Their baptisms were temporary washings that they repeated, sometimes daily, for the repentance (washing of) sins as you read in John 1:24–28 and Acts 19:3–5. Jesus's baptism ushers a new reality: Jesus Christ has conquered sin and death, and a new life in God is possible! Baptism itself does not literally save you; Christ's death and being raised from death saves you from being separated from God forever (Romans 5:9–10). The global church has practiced two kinds of baptism, sprinkling (as babies) and dunking (as adults and older children), and those differ based on two understandings of theology and what God means in baptism. You'll learn more about that later as it's rather involved.

Initially, circumcision was the sign of one's faith in God (Genesis 17:10–11). That practice, meant to be one's physical marking of something spiritual, became merely cultural, so much so that folks were warned *not* to trust that being Jewish (circumcised as Abraham's heir) would save them (Romans 2:28, 29; 3:9, 30). Such brilliant verses! Circumcision has always been about a circumcision of the heart (Deuteronomy 10:16; Romans 2:29). Sons born to Jewish families were circumcised at eight days old; Gentiles who converted to Judaism were often circumcised as adults. Circumcision, a literal cutting, is a symbol, a sign, that the individual and God were making a covenant—a binding promise—of loyalty to the other, one we find through history that humanity usually broke and God upheld. Baptism signals something new. Through his work on the cross, God made a way for us to relate to him by his Spirit through our belief in what Jesus has done. Think Dr. Who. His regenerations, sort of, picture this change. Baptism symbolizes your rebirth.

Some Christian traditions perform infant baptism, which communicates the family's belief that God has sealed this child for salvation and their commitment to likewise raise that child. Other Christians practice adult baptism, where you publicly testify what you think about

God in your life, like you would in a group meeting, at an interview, or a press conference. It gives someone a chance to show the world, "Hey, I believe in what Jesus Christ has done for me, pictured here. I want to follow him. I am his. Who I was has died. I have been reborn to a new life now." Romans 6 describes it well.

You have been washed clean forever and made new,

Jenny

What Do You Believe?

1. What is baptism?

2. What does baptism picture?

3. Why does it matter?

Notes:

Communion

Dear Beloved of God,

What is one thing that everyone does? What do most people like to do together?

Eat! No matter what culture, no matter what background or identity, social status or political leaning, everyone eats. Eating, at the most basic level of human need, is what all share in common. It is one of everyone's favorite life activities to enjoy together. Sharing food, sharing life.

There's another kind of sharing food and sharing life that happens when the church meets together: the taking of holy communion. What is communion? It is a practice that Jesus told us to begin (Matthew 26:26–28; 1 Corinthians 11:23–26). It is a memorial service of sorts. We take some form of bread and wine (or grape juice) to commemorate what they picture. The bread represents Christ's body that was mutilated, and the wine represents Christ's blood that poured from his body (Luke 22:44). Christians differ over their meaning and form, but with these two items, we remember, confess, and worship.

We remember. Communion recalls the most gruesome event in history; why remember such violence? To remember what unreachable lengths God went to save us. God in Christ was willingly abused for us to accomplish the most amazing feat. God allowed himself to be killed to conquer evil and our death. We also remember the depth of evil that spins from our hearts daily, birthed in thought and acted out through our mouths, hands, and bodies. In communion, we remember that God should not be taken for granted nor his grace taken advantage (1 Corinthians 11:27–32).

We confess. In remembering ways that we specifically have turned from God, we are given an opportunity to confess these to God. Of course, God knows these already. Confession is for our sake. It is a chance to be honest, brutally. For all the ways we hide on a daily basis, communion is one time where our heads are bowed, and our hearts are bared. It can be ugly, but confession frees us. Confession lets our consciences breathe freely again. Confession lets God forgive us (1 John 1:8–10).

As an aside, I don't understand why people in Protestant churches are not more focused during communion. Many tend to talk, fidget, look around, shuffle. Are you kidding me? Of all places, over Christ's body and blood, this is one of the few times we could be the least distracted to actually take account of our lives and confess our sins! OK, that was a bit of rant, but seriously, I think we've simply lost a sense of the weight of our sins. They are heavy, like a gabillion tons on top of our hearts extinguishing the life right out of us. And like many things in the U.S., it's easy to take communion for granted. It's no big deal, right?

IT IS A HUGE DEAL. Communion pictures the indescribable love God has for us. If that doesn't fill you every time so that you explode in worship, there's some more confessing to do. I'm not saying there's some special feeling you must have every time, but it is a holy act of worship. Since communion is to be celebrated consistently (1 Corinthians 11:26), many times taking communion will find us grieved, despairing, angry, frozen, or in any one of a host of emotional states. Being a Christian is not about faking a smile. It's about worshipping God as honestly as you can. It's difficult to quiet our hearts in this crazy world. Our hearts harden (Psalm 95:7–11; Hebrews 3:7–13). We let resentment, bitterness, envy, and hopelessness drain us. Scripture shows us that your heart is the fountain of your life (Proverbs 4:23). Let that dry up, and it is game over. It's so easy to accuse God, to not believe that God is good, to think that God isn't doing this or that for us, to lose faith in God. Communion is one time where we ask God to pump the lifeblood of faith back into our brittle hearts. For what purpose? To remain tender enough to worship the one true God. God is worthy of all the honor, credit, and respect that you can give him.

Of all the ways to remember Christ's death and resurrection, God chose eating and drinking. That's important. Eating together is one of the most common and intimate forms of life together. Communion comes from the Latin word, *communio*, meaning a mutual participation, something all share in common when they take part. Despite all the illegitimate power structures currently in place in our world, despite the constant prejudice that runs through our veins, in that moment of taking communion, all around the world, people are equals at the base of that rugged cross—human and broken and lost without God.

Sharing together,

Jenny

What Do You Believe?

1. Why would Jesus ask you to remember his death?

2. What do you need to confess to God before you next take communion?

3. What does communion have to do with suffering?

Notes:

Part Two:

Living Like a Christian

8

Choices

Dear Follower of the Way,[14]

Remember, it is important to find someone to disciple you and help you mature in the Christian faith. Also remember that this person is flawed, so ultimately, you have to take responsibility for your own decisions. If I could boil down what you will face in life each day as a Christian, it is this:

In this situation, will you choose life or choose death?
God or not God?

This relates to whether you are making the simplest decisions or the toughest ones, in whatever situation you find yourself. Read Deuteronomy 30. You might start with Chapter 29 where God gives a great review of events. God has made it plain from the beginning that what we choose, and how we act matters. It brings death or life.

You have decided to follow Jesus, so what does that look like every day? It means that the way you make decisions has changed. It may mean the choices you make change but not necessarily. Now, you look at the heart of the matter, your motivation, and how this will play out long-term. You are thinking in terms of what will honor

God. Once you determine that, then the choice before you remains: which will you choose?

This does not mean that you agonize over every choice. Imagine you have a package of M&M's in front of you. There may be a moral choice in deciding whether or not to eat them. Say you were a diabetic. What should your choice be? Say M&M's are your personal trigger to binge. Say eating M&Ms is a fond memory of sharing them with your grandfather, or you simply desire a treat from the bowl at a party. Lots of reasons could determine whether one should or should not eat said M&Ms in that moment. I'm pretty sure God will not care whether you eat the green or the blue ones. I call these right or left decisions, rather than right or wrong decisions. This is a silly example, I know, but the reason behind the act is what matters most to God. Why are you doing it? How are you doing it? Some choices, between choices that bring life or those that bring death, are the same for most everyone. Many choices, however, will differ among people based on their own hearts and personal circumstances. Sometimes, you'll choose not to do something that you personally feel is no problem to do, simply for the sake of another person (Romans 14).

Following Jesus means choosing what he would choose. What honors God? Again, once you determine that in a given situation, then the choice before you remains: which will you choose? Once you know, then the hard work becomes choosing it! Read 2 Corinthians 10:5. This is such a practical verse. God knows we will struggle to make the right choice, especially the harder the choice is. This verse teaches us that the freedom to choose the best starts in your head. What are you thinking? Those thoughts are what need to change, each one being brought to obey Christ, to match what God says on the matter.

This takes slowing down, listening, thinking, asking, considering, but it'll be worth it to you. Always. Here are some questions to ask yourself:

- Is God asking me to do this?
- What has God already said about this?
- Will doing this bring me closer to Jesus?
- Will doing this get in the way of following Jesus?
- What am I really wanting?

Now choose life,

Jenny

What Do You Believe?

1. What is the last thing God told you to do? Did you do it?

2. What do you need to walk away from?

3. This week, what do you personally need to walk toward?

Notes:

9

Contradictions

Dear Christian,

Remember in high school when we learned the term paradox in our English class? Paradox, an apparent contradiction, crosses our path each day. A personal order of a latte with non-fat milk, sugar-free syrup, no whip, and a huge chocolate chip cookie. A cardiovascular nurse who smokes. The Pope yelling at parishioners. A poor person giving generously. God being killed.

Paradox is one of my favorite ways to describe the Christian life. Following Christ sometimes means doing the opposite of what everyone else is doing. Read these verses to see if you know what I mean and if you agree.

- Job 13:15
- 1 Corinthians 1:25, 27
- 1 Peter 2:21–24

What paradoxes do you notice?

The Puritans in the 1600s touched on the paradox of the Christian life.[15] Here is a bit from one of their prayers (rephrased for clarity):[16]

Lord, high and holy, meek and lowly,
You have brought me to the valley of vision,
    where I live in the deep,

but see You in the heights;
hemmed in by mountains of sin,
   I see Your glory.
Let me learn by paradox
  that the way down is the way up,
  that to be low is to be high,
  that the broken heart is the healed heart,
  that the contrite spirit is the joyful spirit,
  that the remorseful soul is the victorious soul,
  that to have nothing is to possess all,
  that to bear the cross is to wear the crown,
  that to give is to receive,
  that the valley is the place of vision.
Lord, in the daytime,
   stars can be seen in the deepest wells,
And the deeper the wells,
   the brighter your stars shine;
Let me find Your light in my darkness,
  Your life in my death,
  Your joy in my sorrow,
  Your grace in my sin,
  Your riches in my poverty
  Your glory in my valley.

So many things seem like contradictions, strange and beautiful, in our Christian faith. To give is better than to receive (Acts 20:35). Strength comes from weakness (2 Corinthians 12:9–10). The best form of power comes by humility (1 Peter 5:6). Dying is living (John 12:24–26). Living is dying (Colossians 3:3). Not everything, of course, is contradictory. The punishment for turning from God is death (Romans 6:23). What you plant, you get (Galatians 6:7). Action brings consequence, as you well know. When it comes to living as a Christian though, much of what you do will be contradictory to how the world chooses to live.

Be a *good* nonconformist (according to Romans 12:1–2),

Jenny

What Do You Believe?

1. What is the hardest contradiction about God or being a Christian at this point for you?

2. What have you seen God help you do in your life that didn't make sense to other people?

3. What are people around you currently doing that you are not? What are you doing that they aren't?

Notes:

10

Failure

Dear Wayward One,

While being a Christian, what happens when you fail to act like a good one? When, not if. When we are reborn, we still have to learn, like a baby, how to hold up our head, how to feed, how to walk, with much stumbling involved. God must reteach us most things about how to think and feel about life (Romans 12:1–2). It's messy. God is so patient with us. Learning to live faithfully as a Christian takes time. That's why you need the Spirit, the Scripture, and the church. You can't do it alone.

Look at this amazing verse, Proverbs 24:16a: "For though a righteous man falls seven times, he rises again." That's us! We fail to live like God. Failure, however, can't be your excuse. For example:

1) Some use the realities of failure and freedom to take advantage of God on purpose. I love that God speaks to that clearly (Romans 6:1–2; 1 Corinthians 15:34; Hebrews 6:4–6). You know, the excuses of "the devil made me do it" or "I'll work on it tomorrow, after I have one last . . ." or "I have needs . . ."

2) Some get stuck in the quicksand of their failures, paralyzing themselves and sabotaging their ability to move forward. Self-focus, or as my husband calls it—navel gazing—needs to be redirected.

3) Some believe the lies that God's enemy sends to destroy them (John 10:10). The devil is not looking out for our best interests, I promise you that, so why do we believe him over what God says about us? Shame is different from guilt; condemnation is different from conviction. More on that in a minute.

Folks in each of these examples make the same mistake. It's not all about us. We should desire to move toward the good to give the full honor that God is due. Failure will happen, but we certainly aren't trying to fail. The danger comes in continuing to intentionally choose other things over God brazenly. We will fight these urges until our re-creation. The issue is not caring and stubbornly walking down the same path when you know it's wrong.

So when you fail, face it honestly and openly. Tell God. Tell those who are walking in the faith with you. Check out 1 John 1:8–10. Even in your sin, when you confess it, you are beautiful—not because you have it all together, but because you don't act like you have it all together! Failure reminds us that we are helpless and need God to live through us every single day.

When you fail, his Spirit will prompt you. The Spirit acts like a gentleman. God doesn't storm in and bully you into obedience, nor does he use what you've done wrong to make you feel worthless. That's evil. You'll sense the difference. If it's from God, you'll have a sense of conviction, sadness, grief, guilt, and a desire to make it right. If it's from the evil one, you'll feel accused, shamed, and condemned in your sense of self-worth or personal value to God. The father of lies, Satan, doesn't use discipline; he shames (John 8:44). Feeling ashamed (because we've done something legitimately wrong against God) is a good thing and very different from being shamed.

God, however, absolutely uses discipline when we fail. Read Hebrews 12:4–13. Discipline calls our failures out on the carpet, to be exposed, to be healed. Discipline restores. It shows us that we are his children. Read Revelation 3:19. What an interesting verse and in the book we might least expect.

When you fail, fall on God's grace.

Then get up, again and again and again.

Love,

Jenny

P.S.

A word on Christian leaders failing. They should know better. Their failures, of all people, remind us not to place them on a pedestal of human fame and show us how desperately important it is that we stay close to God and his people daily not to get off track. The enemy, like a viper before its strike, is coiled and ready, waiting for any opportunity to ruin our lives (1 Peter 5:8).

What Do You Believe?

1. In what area(s) have you fallen the most?

2. Why?

3. Do you believe that God is for you no matter what? Why or why not?

Notes:

11

Gifting

Dear Gift of God,

When God formed each of us, he was intentional. God knew what the world needed when he made you, and he gave you special gifts to give back to this world.

This starts at birth. Read Psalm 119:73–74 and Psalm 139:13–16.

This continues at rebirth. When you responded in faith to God's call to be saved and changed, God's Spirit gifted you in a new way. God gifts each believer spiritually to benefit the church. Read 1 Peter 4:10. What qualifies as a spiritual gift? Paul gives examples, so read the verses in Romans 12:6–8 and 1 Corinthians 12:8–10.

What does this mean for you? It means that from birth and from rebirth, God wants to work through you to bless, to nurture, to bring light, to expose darkness.

Some wonder whether spiritual gifts are skills or passions. I say yes. At your physical birth, he instilled in you natural gifts and talents and passions. At your spiritual rebirth, God designed you to be spiritually gifted. Are these talents and passions ever the same? Maybe. You will know your spiritual gifting by the energy in which is done (by the Spirit in your effort) and the supernatural, inexplicable results for good that come from it. You will need to develop it, but when you are operating from your spiritual gift(s), I believe that in those moments you will feel most fully alive when you are using them for the good of the church.

Others can often help you see your spiritual gifting better than you might see it, so ask other Christians, "What do you see me doing within the church that God blesses?" or "What am I passionate to do in church?" You see, God has gifted you for the church, to build it up. So while your passion and skill might be used in everyday life, your spiritual gifting will be best demonstrated within the church. One last thing: spiritual gifts aren't necessarily dramatic. They can be, but sometimes they quietly usher in the kingdom of God.

For example, I have been vocally trained to sing, but I am not passionate about it, nor am I particularly gifted, in my opinion (sorry, Mum). I also am gifted in administrative tasks that I use to full measure professionally and personally, but I don't particularly enjoy them. They are more of a duty, a chore. I naturally can administer, but it does not bring me joy. Now might one have the natural gift of administration and the spiritual gift of administration? Yes, but perhaps not necessarily. As a Christian, I need to ask myself, "What brings me joy?" as well as "In what am I skilled that demonstrates good for God's people?" You're looking for both in order to understand your spiritual gift(s). You'll know your gift by this: when you give it, you are energized despite the hard work it requires (all other things being equal, e.g. getting enough rest and eating properly). You are filled as you pour out. I'm curious. What do you think your spiritual gifting is?

Live your gift,

Jenny

P.S.

Because all have been created by God, many manage huge accomplishments. Sometimes the biggest haters of God will still use the incredible talent he has given them. It's just that all of these deeds won't matter in the end because they weren't done from love for God. Deeds done with the wrong motivations will burn in the end (1 Corinthians 3:11–15).

What Do You Believe?

1. What natural skills and talents has God given you?

2. What spiritual gifts has God given you for the good of the church?

3. What might you need to give up in order to have time to use your spiritual gift(s)?

Notes:

12

Generosity

Dear Blessing,

Being generous. Let me write first: you probably already do this better than I. Generosity is a sweet fragrance of love, and I pray that you live out Psalm 119:99 every day.

So what does generosity have to do with living like a Christian?

Everything.

When we understand what God has given to us, why are we holding anything back from others? Yes, you need to be faithful to care for your family. Yes, you should save for retirement if you can. But boy, have we mastered how not to give! Generosity has long been a sign of a faithful follower of God and just as long been a struggle for most (think Cain, Jonah, that mother in 1 Kings 3:16–26, Ananias and Sapphira, various church leaders in our lifetime, etc.).

What do you give? Your time, your talents, your resources, your story, and your spirit. Share with others whatever God has given you.

Which of these you give will vary by season of life. Do not beat yourself up over what you can't give during certain periods of life. Just make sure you are generous in multiple ways all the time. This will almost always be best demonstrated by what slips from your mouth. When people meet you, you want them to see Jesus's compassion, purity, simplicity, and precision in getting to the heart of things.

Read Ephesians 5:1–2. Imitate God's generosity. That's an incredible command. Be fragrant. Be sweet-smelling. When I am rude to someone (yes, it happens—too often!), I imagine how that must have smelled. Like rotten garbage? Like flesh rotting? It's disgusting when we are not generous because it stinks. Instead of lightening a person's burden that day through our generosity, we've increased it. And most people are pretty weighed down enough already, carrying a heavy load of guilt, shame, fear, and pain.

God generously reaches us through our physiological senses, and thank God! His generosity flows to us through the splendors in our human existence. Beauty is seen, heard, smelled, felt, etc. I appreciate art because any of its forms (music, sculpture, mimes, flash mobs, street art, calligraphy, and more) teaches me about the stunning beauty God has allowed us to have and reminds me to be generous.

You are God's perfume (2 Corinthians 2:15),

Jenny

What Do You Believe?

1. Read what Jesus says in Matthew 6:19–34 and how he connects faith to giving, contrasted by fear.

2. Read James 1:9–12, and consider how these verses relate to you today.

3. Generosity is not just about money, so in what ways/areas do you struggle to be generous?

Notes:

13

Goodness

Dear Saint,

God coined the word holiness (Leviticus 11:44–45; 19:2; 20:7; 1 Peter 1:16), but I'm trying to think of a word that might relate more to us in the twenty-first century. How about goodness? Holiness means being without fault, like a gorgeous gem without imperfection. Businesses strive to produce a perfect diamond, so we get what perfection means. But when it comes to our human behavior, we're ok with being so-so. It's curious and sad. Innocence and goodness are close playmates, so you may see a few connections from my latter letter to you.

Vice. Virtue. These are age-old church words. We can list our vices easily. What about our virtues?

Virtue. I love this word. It's our basis for a code of ethics in law and life. Lose virtue, and we can pretty much do as we please. The fallout wouldn't concern us.

God deserves our goodness, and, in fact, can demand it. If we are God's creatures and went AWOL on God, wouldn't we be held accountable? Our basic instinct is that some things are wrong, and some things are right. People don't agree on which is which, but few are debating that wrong—a sense of what not to do at times—does not exist.

God calls us, as his creatures, to be good. Goodness is a willingness for God's ways; however, each of us has opened wide the door of our hearts to welcome in evil. Many times. Even now as Christians, we cave sometimes. Your spirit is ready, but your flesh is feeble (Matthew 26:41; Mark 14:38). In other words, the Spirit of God within you is strong and wills to obey God, but sin—think of sin as cancer cells corrupting your body—has attacked your body and made it weak. You know when you get so tired that you can hardly hold your eyes open, much less make an informed decision? Many of us, even as Christians, are so tired from sin that I wonder if we are sleepwalking through life.

Goodness takes effort and energy. The habits I write about later will strengthen your spirit to enable you to be alert to obey God in the moment that you are challenged. God will always be there to help you to be able to choose the good (1 Corinthians 10:13; 2 Peter 1:3–4), but if and when you do not, it's not God's fault (James 1:13–15). We choose evil. God is the One stepping in to help us to *be able to* choose goodness at all.

For all our opportunities to disobey in life—our parents, God, laws, experimenting just to say we did—do we ever talk about disobeying evil? God allows one disobedience and that is to deny—to disobey—our physical body's instincts and urges that it is screaming at us to fulfill.

Throughout history, unrestrained sexuality has demonstrated one of the most common ways we have opposed God's demand for holiness (Baal worship in 2000 B.C. and Rome in the first century, for example). In our twenty-first century, sex-obsessed culture, one might think nothing can beat our uninhibited, unrestrained sexual expression. Remember, God gave us freedom to be chained to Christ and to be his servant, not to do whatever we want.

The other side of self-indulgence—unwarranted restraint—is no better. We hop between letting it all go or holding it all in. In both, we miss the point. God doesn't want us to settle for either extreme. Extreme restraint may appear to "deny the flesh" but actually does not tame it.[17] Repression can cheat you as much as full expression! Just watch the scene in the movie, *Chocolat*, when the legalistic mayor absolutely loses it in that storefront window of chocolate. The point is that God's rules are for good reason. We absolutely should follow them, but following all the rules does not a good woman make (Romans 3:19–20; Galatians 3:21–24). So much more to say here on the flesh, but I have to get back to goodness.

Goodness is something God enables you to be: unselfish, pure, teachable, ready, open, sacrificial, slow to speak, slow to anger, loving. It's a miracle every time we choose the good.

Choose goodness and live,

Jenny

What Do You Believe?

1. Can you be good? Read Psalms 14:1–3; 53:1–3; Ecclesiastes 7:20; Romans 3:10–12, 23.

2. Why does God expect us to be good?

3. What do you struggle with more—being too unrestrained or too restrictive?

4. What will goodness look like for you this week?

Notes:

14

Identity

Dear Believer in Jesus,

Becoming a Christian changes who you are (2 Corinthians 5:17). Like a caterpillar that becomes a butterfly, you are reborn. Your sense of identity becomes subject to your identity in Christ (Galatians 2:20). This rupture involves a departing and binding, exchanging and adopting, distancing and embracing, an altering and preserving of who you thought you were. Each conception you hold of yourself must be re-evaluated in light of your new identity (Romans 6:1–7, 20–22; 1 Corinthians 6:9–12).

Who we were is not lost but redeemed. Our individuality is not abandoned, as if erased, but not everything with which we identify is godly. Being remade into the likeness of Christ requires you to be someone who you were not (Romans 12:1–2; Ephesians 4:23–24; Colossians 3: 9–10; 1 John 3:3). Some of your previous opinions about yourself will be proved true while other self-identifications, once thought precious, will be disrupted (1 Corinthians 3:9–15; 13:12; 1 John 2:17; 3:2). One's transformation as a believer in Christ means a reordering of one's identities.[18]

You do not know who you are or who you should be. Why? Because we were born into this world divided in our bodies and psyches. That we are born broken (sinful) is called "original sin." Not all of our desires are pure because sin corrupted our desires, plus we are easily deceived. Sin has darkened and disoriented our human understanding, yet, in our arrogance, we give ourselves too much credit! Humanity lost its true identity since the first couple in the Garden of Eden (Genesis 3). Most of what we know is a re-gurgitation of whatever cultural messages were drilled into our minds through various media and entertainment. Learning to love and follow Christ—that is, becoming his disciple—is the remaking of our identity, and God gave us the Spirit, the church, and the Bible to guide us.

We question cultural messages (whether common or "Christian"), reconciling them with what God has already said about our identity in Christ. Read Romans 12:1–2, Ga-latians 3:27, and Colossians 3:9–10 again. As an example, identifying with a certain ethnic group is not necessarily sinful. Prioritizing it over your common identity with oth-ers in Christ is. Dressing ourselves in identity is a great image. Humanly defined identities are optional. They are changeable. As the verses say, think about being covered in Christ rather than anything else as you get dressed in the morning. Who you are is who you are in Christ. That's your truest identity.

You first came to Christ because you were convicted that you were not right and wanted to change. Now be very brave and let God re-form you.

Love,

Jenny

What Do You Believe?

1. What have other people told you that you are?

2. Who do you think you were?

3. Who do you think you are?

Notes:

15

Innocence (Holiness)

Dear Cleansed,

You're amazing, you know that? You give much to many. Your heart is tender and teachable. Your smile rushes into the room to welcome others. You own your mistakes and keep moving forward. I wish I could watch you grow as you walk in faith. Living as a Christian does not mean you will be perfect; in fact, you will not be, but Jesus calls us to "be innocent" (Matthew 10:16).

Ponder for a moment what that means.

Innocence to me is crisp white linen that has just been laundered. It's fresh. It's fragrant. It's light. Pure. Good. Who really wants to be a soiled, smelly rag?

I use the word innocence for its familiarity, not its exactness (Isaiah 64:6). Because we have sinned, we don't return to a state of innocence like Adam and Eve possessed originally. We still feel the sting of sin, pain, and death now. So while we are cleansed, made righteous, as if we were innocent, we are not. The innocence we pursue now is holiness, living a pure life according to God (Leviticus 11:44–45; Matthew 5:48; 1 Peter 1:15–17).

Think about what our culture prizes. Being provocative. How much will we spend to be provocative? What could we flaunt to be provocative? How far could we go to be provocative? What new limit could be pushed to be provocative? It seems everyone is trying to be provocative in a bad way. But who's being provocative about being good? Being innocent and changing the world to be a better place? I say to you, be provocatively good. That takes a ton more imagination and effort!

There's a reason why movies and media showcase gore and sex. It tempts. It entices. It sells. Mark God's words, though. Somebody always pays (Galatians 6:7–9; James 2:12). Temptations can differ by culture, and our North American world at present seems to be most absorbed in making money, exploiting sex, and seeking self-fulfillment no matter the cost.

You have been washed clean—symbolized in baptism—to live a changed life, a new life of holiness. New. Fresh. Crisp. Happy. Like bright linen. So it makes sense why Jesus would command us not to live like everyone else. Make different choices. Make provocative choices.

Rise above,

Jenny

What Do You Believe?

1. Take a moment for confession. Reflect on your last few days, and tell God where you have blown it. Part of being innocent is being painfully honest.

2. Reread Matthew 10:16, and consider what Jesus says about the snake and dove. Why would he use those to picture what he calls you to be?

3. How can you practice being innocent this week in a way you were not so last week?

Notes:

16

Intimacy

Dear Irreplaceable,

Think about a comrade-in-arms. Someone who is there for you through thick and thin. Someone who goes to battle with you and for you. My husband calls me his battle companion. That's a window into what intimacy means.

Can true intimacy only be found through a sexual relationship in marriage? What about those who are widowed or single or divorced or disabled? It seems we've wedged intimacy into this tiny box and cheated ourselves. Think about it. God designed you to belong to him and to others. That connectedness, that belonging, empowers you. We talk about human instincts and drives—well, that is one. God designed a different intimacy in marriage, but it's not as if he left everyone else out to dry. Whether single or married, in each stage of life, you can and should find intimacy. Intimacy is defined as closeness, familiarity, a confidence with another, togetherness.

Intimacy is a chance to have another person who knows you so closely, so deeply, that you are able to bare your soul to them without fear in complete honesty. To be psychologically and emotionally naked, so to speak, with someone safe. This is healthy. This is needed. Because intimacy is raw exposure, you cannot be intimate with everyone, nor too soon with those you choose. This takes time and trust to build and should be mutual. And it's not primarily about romantic interest. Sam and Frodo in *The Lord of the Rings* are a great example of intimacy in friendship. Consider how the team members on *Scorpion* Season 1 relate, as they slowly grow in intimacy. Or take Mary and Tom in *Downton Abbey* as siblings-in-law.

God gave us each a family, friends, and a church to experience this amazing connection. Some of us did not experience much intimacy through our biological families, so we find others to fill that void. You might count your sisters and your best friend as intimates. And perhaps your spiritual mother. Watch, however, which friendships you create and with whom. Intimacy is soul-baring, so one can easily get swept up into illegitimate romance.

So you have this need to be known. This is a good thing. You just have to be careful who you let know you, for real. Of course, God wants to be intimate with you most of all.

God's amazing grace and peace and love are yours,

Jenny

What Do You Believe?

1. Who would you name as your intimates?

2. With whom should you not be intimate?

3. What boundaries should you have to protect yourself against the wrong person becoming too intimate with you?

4. Intimacy involves physical touch but need not be sexual. What's the difference?

Notes:

17

Joy

Dear Lover of Life,

Jesus came to bring us life and not just forever life with him after death. He was raised to bring us a new life in this world (John 3:17; 10:10). God forgives, frees, restores, and heals us (Psalm 103:1–18). So why don't Christians look more happy?

That is our indictment! We should be the most light-hearted, the quickest to smile or laugh, the slowest to condemn. Is the problem what we fix our eyes and hearts on (2 Corinthians 4:18; Hebrews 12:2)? If we are looking for a job transfer, more hair, less hair, a new spouse, etc. to be happy, if we are expecting our situation to change to bring us joy, we will be disappointed.

Many things bring us pleasure, certainly. Receiving a year-end bonus, watching our children succeed, or accomplishing an item on our bucket list, for example, are fulfilling. However, the joy we have as Christians comes from our relationship with God. Our joy is in God (Nehemiah 8:10; Philippians 4:4). Moreover, everything about God and from God should fill us with satisfaction. Loving all that God has made, we delight in the softness of a puppy's fur, a boldly-colored cardinal, unique architecture, a new science discovery, humor, exploring, embracing, or any host of things that come our way. We enjoy everything that God has gifted to us.

The joy we have in God shines through us (Matthew 5:14–16). If we stay focused on who God is and all that God has done for us, we would be more cheerful, less worrisome, faster to applaud any bright moment, the most optimistic, knowing that God does incredible things (Psalm 57:2; 2 Corinthians 2:14). Are we waiting for God to do what we want for our joy to start? We have joy because we know God! Even writing that sentence stops me. I am overcome with amazement to think that God cares about me and you. God is for us (Romans 8:31). What more could we want? There are a great many things we will want, and that is not wrong; it's more about our perspective when we do not receive them. It's human to want food, water, shelter, love, provision, and many in our world are suffering without these. (We should help, by the way; see my letter on justice.) One of my lessons as a Christian was learning from my Christian friends from Haiti when we were students together. I saw a brightness in their eyes and a laughter in their soul that I had not met before. I asked them about it, and they offered, "Most Haitians live in poverty, and that is very difficult, but their joy is in God. How can we not sing when we know God?"

Finding a constant joy in Jesus does not mean ignoring the ills of the world. Far from looking the other way or denying what's happening, Christians should be deeply invested in what God cares about—the world and everything in it (John 3:16)! Romans 12:15 gives us a wonderful balance: we cheer with those who celebrate and mourn with those who grieve. We better not spout off annoying clichés to those who are hurting or offer some "at least you … "

advice (watch Brené Brown's three-minute clip on empathy). We would offer the anchor of hope that is God our Savior (Psalm 25:5; 61:2; Hebrews 6:18–19).

Joyfully,

Jenny

P.S.

A danger lies in trying to force God into a corner about a given point in time. In other words, do we expect God to have to act in a given circumstance? We, of course, ask and believe that God can and will do what we ask, according to God's will. But how well do we understand God's will (Isaiah 55:8–9; Romans 11:33–34; James 4:3; 1 John 5:14–15)? Why was my friend's child taken by cancer at age five? Why did my husband suffer a difficult childhood? Why have I experienced the treasure of my parents remaining married while so many others have had to grow up bouncing between homes and holiday meals? While the evil one rules this present life, we do suffer (John 16:33; 1 John 5:19).

What Do You Believe?

1. Where do you find joy?

2. When you struggle to find joy, why? What else is going on?

3. Who can you help this week who is struggling?

Notes:

18

Judging

Dear Truth-teller,

A word on judging.

Read the story of the prodigal son in Luke 15:11–32, and watch how the older brother behaves. Often, our judgments passed on other people are more about our own resentment, jealousy, hypocrisy, and self-deception with which we have not dealt. So deal before you judge. Analyze your own heart. That's #1. Read Jesus's caution directed to the religious hypocrites of his day in Matthew 7:1–5.

Secondly, we have no business judging those who do not claim faith in Jesus Christ (1 Corinthians 5:12–13). It's between them and God. So all the verbal comments, Facebook posts, tweets, and texts trying to make some snarky point about how non-Christians should be behaving make me cringe. That's not our job. They are entitled to their own opinions. Why? Because God gives them this freedom. Why is our response not to love and pray for them? It's mind-boggling. Instead, because we don't like this or that they are doing or believe, we judge. That, my friend, is on us.

If others ask our opinion, we may graciously share our personal views. This is best done in the context of a personal relationship with them. This means they've personally known us for a while, and an established trust and rapport has been built with them *before* discussing a hot topic. Otherwise, it might be better to hold our tongue. Being able to hear the truth depends on the context, environment, and spirit in which it is offered. So #3, in what spirit are you speaking the truth?

That said, some may think there's no place for judging. Uhhmmm. Most everyone judges what they think is wrong (the acts, not the people committing them). That's how we as a society decide what is illegal. Judgment is necessary to name those evils that harm the vulnerable.

Also, certain parties do rightfully judge. Here are some examples of legit judging:

- God with us.
- An authority with its subject.
- Parents with their children.
- HR with their employees.
- Teachers grading assignments.
- "Friends don't let friends drive drunk."
- An equestrian and the horse.
- The church with its members.
- Christians in your circle who have given you the right to judge them.

So #4, there is a valid and necessary place for judging each other as Christians, within the local and worldwide church. Individual Christians are accountable to the larger body of Christ. We're all supposed to be working together toward one end (Christlikeness), not going in whichever direction we like. Paul makes this clear in 1 Corinthians 5:9–13. See what Jesus says in John 7:24. Some who think they are Christians will be horrifically surprised based on what Jesus says in Matthew 7:21–23. A person's actions do reflect what they believe about God and may indicate that they are *not* God's (Matthew 7:15–20; 1 John 2:3–6, 9–11); however, this is very hard to judge from our perspective tied to a specific point in time, so proceed slowly with extreme caution.

Judgmentalism (what we most often do, wrongly) is different from making an appropriate judgment. For example, if your three-year-old daughter wanted to cross the street with abandon, it's not like you would stand idly by, exclaiming, "You do you!" Certain things are life-threatening, unhealthy, or unholy, and because of our sincere love for another, we speak into each other's lives. There are those, then, at times whom we should judge (ourselves and those who claim fellowship with us in Christ) and others whom we personally are not to judge (basically, everyone else). There is a right way to judge and a wrong way. So when someone asks you, "Should Christians judge?," the answer is, "Well, that depends . . ."

Wanting the best for you,

Jenny

What Do You Believe?

1. Read and compare John 7:24 and 1 Samuel 16:7 (and their surrounding verses to understand the background of the story). What about being human makes our judgments so "off" so often?

2. What have you left unjudged in your own life?

3. Have you avoided sharing the truth with someone, with whom you do have the permission and respect to speak into their life?

Notes:

19

Justice

Dear Justice-seeker,

By justice, I am referring to the part we play in God's justice. God is putting the world back to right and has invited us to be on the team of Project Earth Restoration (Genesis 1:28; Isaiah 11; Acts 3:19–21; 2 Corinthians 5:17–10; Ephesians 4:29–24; Revelation 21:1–10; 22:3). God will right every wrong done and restore the world. Christians should be leading the charge on cultural care (for others, for creatures, for the earth). By charge, I do not mean wielding physical weapons or protecting the privileges that Christians may have once had, as a cultural majority power in the U.S. Bringing God's justice is not about protecting our turf as I have written about elsewhere; it is about sharing, risking, giving, loving, opening ourselves to others. This is a holy cause but somehow, as can happen, we take the matters into our own hands and twist it into a skewed crusade. Even while we intend to help, we harm. This is why seeking justice is so important to do in community, in communion. Christianity, remember, is a team sport. At the moment, I especially like what I see coming from those in the (&) Campaign (theandcampaign.com). Seeking "redemptive justice," they are committed to biblical truth, civic engagement, and political participation in seeking to bring community transformation. What a fantastic example of what we should be doing! Let's be the woman who hid a defenseless baby (Exodus 1:22; 2:3), a housemaid who spoke up to save her captor (2 Kings 5:2–3), the White Rose students who defied Nazism and paid for it, or the ones who marched from Selma to Montgomery. Let's care for our neighbors in a way that restores the world.

What types of issues do I mean? The issues vary by time period and culture, but many result from human greed, fear, and the misuse of power. A natural disaster can also devastate a population that would call for Christian care and service, such as the bubonic plague that devastated Asia, Africa, and Europe in the 14th century or the earthquakes and tsunamis that hit Southeast Asia (2004) and Japan (2011). More often, evil is brought by our own hands. For example, group conflict resulted in the Rwandan genocide (1994), and most, if not all, nations have experienced political corruption at the highest levels of government like Brazil, Russia, or the U.S.

Facing racism, sexism, homophobia (or fear of any different you-name-it), gun violence, terrorism, denial of human rights, drug and sex trafficking should be at the forefront of our minds. What part as Christians are we playing right now to right these wrongs? What are we doing to care for the poor, the disadvantaged, disabled, mentally ill, foreigners, widows, orphans, single parents— physically, spiritually, emotionally, financially (Leviticus 19:34; Matthew 25:35; James 1:26–27). If our faith in Christ is real, it moves us to act. God will one day end evil and address all the wrongs done on the earth, ultimately

(Exodus 3:7–10; Psalm 34:17). We are to live as resurrection people now in light of that future.

Keep bringing light to the world,

Jenny

What Do You Believe?

1. Why would God involve us in the earth's restoration?

2. What is going on in the world that most breaks your heart?

3. What good can you do today for someone else?

Notes:

20

Loyalty (Love)

Dear Mirror to God,

I am not your best example for a demonstration of loyalty, but I can share some thoughts on the matter as I strive to be. Of all Jesus's disciples, of all who numbered the crowds, of all those healed by his words and hands, who was standing with Christ at his greatest display of love for us as he suffered and died? Of all Jesus's followers, who stood with him when the chips were down, when it looked like all hope was lost? As far as is accounted, one man and mostly women, as my husband pointed out once. Isn't that interesting? Few of us are loyal. Few of us love. That's why we need God's Spirit every day to be different people.

Loyalty has to do with love. Loyalty is about living in such a way that honors and respects the people around us and ourselves. Loyalty drives the choices you make to protect the other. For example:

- Your choice of words in a situation. Do they speak life or death into it?
- What you wear. Does it honor and protect those around you?
- How you spend your time. Does it prioritize what God wants for you?
- With whom you are close. Do your friends help you (1 Corinthians 15:33)?

- Where your eyes roam. Enough said.
- The state of our heart. Is it hard? Brittle? Alive?
  Crushed? Warm? Closed? Full?

The heart of the matter is, actually, your heart. It is the well that waters your entire existence (Proverbs 4:23). It is the fountain that spouts grace or spews criticism, love or contempt (Matthew 12:34; 15:10–20; Luke 6:45). It will not do both in any given moment. That is why being aware of what is happening inside your heart each day—and dealing with it—will free you to be loyal, to love.

Hesed is a Hebrew word that fabulously captures how God always behaves toward us: loyal love. Of all the letters I could write on the rules you should follow, I summarize them as Jesus did. Love God with everything we have and love others, like we take care of ourselves (Deuteronomy 6:5–6; Mark 12:30–31). We all have areas of self-loathing; however, we also remain consistently loyal to ourselves. We look after ourselves. So do that for others—as Christ (God) has loved us. That is the new law of love (John 13:34). Love fulfills the law (Romans 13:10). That is loyalty.

For all the lies, gossip, and corners we cut to serve ourselves on a daily basis, God is asking us to demonstrate a love that is loyal to others. It means staying when you want to run. It means waiting and not doing something that seems amazing. It means embracing life by accepting death (the death of your wish of how things would go in the matter). This is hard. It will cost. The thing is, accepting salvation is easy (at least in this country). Following Christ—becoming his disciple—is pricey (Luke 14:25–33). Why? Because love is always obedience to Christ. It will be worth it in the end, but on the way there will be a mountainous hike with plenty of peaks, valleys, and plateaus. If you find yourself floating along easily as a Christian, stop and ask yourself, "When's the last time I was loyal?"

With admiration for you,

Jenny

What Do You Believe?

1. What's going on in your heart this week?

2. In what situations are you struggling to be loyal?

3. How has God shown his loyal love to you recently?

Notes:

21

Respect

Dear Pearl,[19]

When I write the word modesty, what comes to your mind?

Moral, stuffy, prudish, buttoned-up? Propriety, beauty, self-respect? If any of the first set of words came to your mind, it shows that you have been culturally socialized, for that is what the world has taught us that modesty is. To withhold from ourselves any physical pleasure is—according to modern culture—damaging. But, is it? Of course, restraint restricts, but that is commonly done. Preparing for a race, cramming for an exam, saving to buy your child a toy—each requires us to deny ourselves in one respect to pursue something else. Remember, we cannot have it all, so what do you want most? Modesty denies us short-lived pleasures, but affords us greater and lengthier pleasures. What the world sells, sells us short (1 John 2:16–17).

You know now, by your own experience, that what you thought it was that you wanted—what seemed shiny and alluring—turned out to be a tarnished piece of scrap. Brooks Williams wrote a little song, "All That is Gold," based on a poem by J. R. R. Tolkien and plays it on his *Back to Mercy* album. Here is the first verse:

All that is gold does not glitter.
All who wander are not lost.
The old that is strong does not wither.
Deep roots are not touched by frost.
From the ashes, a fire shall be awoken
A light from these shadows shall spring.

Sometimes what you grew up believing turns out to be rubbish. We may have been taught that being modest was a bad thing. Modesty can refer to your appearance, but it also relates to your heart attitude, your motivations of why you are doing this or that. Modesty, being humble and not thinking too highly of yourself than you ought, has to do with respect (Romans 12:3; Philippians 2:3–4).

There's self-respect, which is respecting yourself. It is also about not taking advantage of others. Then there's respect for other creatures and taking care of our good earth. You may have been raised well with respect to the last two, so let me touch on the first and another.

Self-respect. How I wish some women had more gumption. Gumption is having a strong sense of what you are—valuable! I love Angela Duckworth's related word: grit. What is valued is respected. Blokes spend hours buffing their sports cars. Palaces are pristinely cleaned before an important visit from royalty. Yet some of us do not respect our own immortal value.

Respect yourself in the way you speak, dress, think, and act (Proverbs 11:22; Proverbs 14:1). Respect others in the way you speak, dress, think, and act. For example, there is a right way to be attractive, even sexually alluring, which also means there's a wrong way. Don't cheapen your beauty. Respect yourself. You are so important.

R-E-S-P-E-C-T . . . Are you singing that song in your head yet? You're welcome.

Then there's respect for God. The biggie! Proverbs 19:23 states, "The fear of the LORD leads to life; then one rests content, untouched by trouble."[20] See also Proverbs 1:7, 8:13, and 9:10. Fearing God means to understand your position in relation to God's; it means to hold toward God a sense of awe, reverence, worship, compliance, and perhaps a wee bit of fright. You see those God visited through his angels recorded in Scripture, and those folks didn't exactly remain calm! Those who rightly know God's place know theirs—bowed and kneeling. Our confidence in approaching God is based on what God has told us: we are lost, but God loves us and actually wants to save us (Hebrews 11:6).

With all my hopes and dreams for your bright future,

Jenny

P.S.
Interestingly, those who respect God often respect themselves and others because they actually believe what God says about them.

What Do You Believe?

1. What did you first think of God, and how do you describe God now?

2. How can you demonstrate respect this week? To whom?

3. Whom do you need to approach to apologize for not respecting them?

Notes:

22

Sexuality

Dear Jewel,

If engaging in sex was how to find happiness, you'd think most everyone would have found happiness by now. That's the funny thing about sex. You can have it a lot and not be any better off.

To love you, I would not lie to you. You will not find love and happiness going about it the wrong way, and God gave really clear directions (Genesis 1:27-28; 2:22-25; Matthew 19:4-6; Romans 1:18-32; 1 Corinthians 7:2; 1 Thessalonians 4:3-8).

Sexuality is about wholeness, purity, and fulfillment. Your sexuality, your sexual being, and your sexual behavior are extremely important to God. You can trust that most will not be talking about what God desires for you. We must seek *that*—God's desire for you—like hunting for wild and amazing treasure, in the quiet and buried places, increasingly obscured by voices shouting that sexuality is strictly personal and individual. Our sexuality is social in nature and not just physical. Many are not asking the right questions when it comes to sexuality. In following Christ, look to ask the right questions—questions like "What is God's plan for my good? How can I glorify him in all I do, including how I use my body?" God will answer.

Sexuality is a precious part of who you are. Through your physical body, God is *saying* something through how he made us as sexual beings. For example, how an unmarried individual (abstaining from any physical act of sexual intimacy) displays his or her sexuality is beautiful and hardly contemplated! It's not as if Jesus was asexual. He lived out his sexuality in a physically celibate and fulfilling way. Or consider that the differentiation and intimacy between a woman and man in marriage pictures something important about God, about Christ and his church. As you know, Christians have sometimes fallen short in how they have talked about and lived out these incredible truths. Mostly, we've imitated those around us without giving much thought to God, love, or sexuality, because most of us just do whatever we want to do. Three words we don't hear combined often are the words "appropriate" next to the words "sexual behavior." Does anything go? What goes? Why or why not? We personally want to decide (control) who we are. At least in Western civilization, the myth of personal self-rule has duped us.

If, as Christians believe, God created us, what role does God play in forming our sexuality? Jesus shares his answer in Mark 10:6. God created binary biological bodies, yet sin's entrance into the world created anomalies in our genetic line so that even our DNA is corrupted. Even still, God formed you, designing your chromosomes and body parts from perfect love.

We may live in the tension of not being whom we want to be, or not getting to do what we want to do, or struggling with what we don't want but have. Most of us living in the 21st century will come to Christ with some significant sexual baggage, wounds, and confusion. We will need for God to teach us how to live sexually pure lives in the training or re-training of our sexual habits. For this, we need guidance from God's Spirit, a local church, family, and friends, probably a counselor, and definitely a dear mentor who's traveled a bit further down the road.

Love,

Jenny

What Do You Believe?

1. What are God's boundaries for our sexual behavior (for our good)?

2. What Do You Believe being created as female means?

3. What areas of your sexuality (biology, being, and/or behavior) do you find easy or difficult to obey God's directions?

Notes:

23

Suffering

Dear Fellow Sufferer,

This early morning, I write something harder to swallow: suffering is a part of the Christian life. Then again, suffering is a part of this life, so I'm not sure why we get so startled when trouble finds us. How do other religions answer the question of human suffering? If all is chance, what do atheists say to a mother whose young child died of cancer at the age of five? For an animist, suffering is what you deserve since you've angered the gods in some way. A traditional Buddhist wants to lose all connection to this life because suffering is not really real. I have found that Christianity gives the most compelling answer, and you must judge for yourself.

Mitali Perkins shares why she converted from Hinduism to Christianity (back story—when she was in high school, her teenage friend was killed in a car accident involving a drunk driver):

> Clayton's death opened my adolescent eyes to a world of suffering. What kind of God would allow this and then, according to Hinduism, reincarnate us into a painful world? . . . A loving God. Human suffering. How can both exist? . . . [Jesus on the cross] was *God* submitting to the four enemies of humanity—pain, grief, evil, and death—in order to destroy them all.

The cross, then is where a loving God and the suffering of humanity could finally be reconciled.[21]

To follow Christ's example means that, in some ways, we also will suffer (Philippians 3:10; 2 Corinthians 1:5). We often balk when hardships come our way. Well, of course, no one wants hardships, but we should be prepared to expect them. Jesus promises us that (John 16:33). Suffering will come, and it stinks.

However, suffering can also be a very special gift for the Christian. Even though suffering was created when Adam and Eve (and we, in turn) gave themselves over to evil (Genesis 3:14–19; Romans 5:12; 1 Corinthians 15:21–22), God uses suffering purposefully. It is amazing. See the life of a man named Joseph (Genesis 37; 39–50) or Esther (Esther 1–9) or Daniel (Daniel 1–6). You will find that God's main characters recorded in Scripture all face suffering, from which God brings greater gain not just for them individually, but for a larger purpose. So when you suffer, keep your eyes on the horizon, looking ahead to what God might be doing through it.

People suffer for a number of reasons, including:

- The natural consequences of one's own bad behavior.
- The consequences of someone else's bad behavior.
- Demonic attacks (Job 1:6–22; 1 Peter 5:6–9).
- Natural disasters.

In this broken world, suffering comes by cruel hearts, others' and our own. Satan (the angel who walked out on God), as the dark ruler of our present world, continues to be a global wrecking ball (Ezekiel 28:11–19; John 12:31; 2 Corinthians 4:4). Remember, humanity succumbed to deceit, gave over rule to the devil, and God's terms allowed it. *We* surrendered the beautiful claim that God gave us to protect and nurture this earth, and we let an evil presence take charge (Genesis 1:26). If this is starting to sound like some Star Wars movie, isn't that curious? The human heart spins similar dramas like the age-old Babylonian story of *The Epic of Gilgamesh* or *Star Wars*, *Lord of the Rings*, *I Am Legend*, *Book of Eli*, *Star Trek*, etc., because the actual story of God—of good and evil, of conflict, judgment, and over-coming—is true and written on our hearts (Ecclesiastes 3:11; Romans 1:20). We can't help but imitate the faint whisper of this supreme story etched on our souls.

God is not evil then to allow the suffering that we bring upon ourselves. What's incredible is that God does not leave us there! He can redeem every moment of our suffering, every tear spilled. Look for him. Redeem is a powerful word that means "to buy back." Think of a slave being bought his or her freedom. God not only fixes everything in the end, but also redeems pain and suffering and uses it for good now. Who else does that?

God does not waste our suffering. What possible good could God bring from our personal anguish? I'll mention a few. It allows us to identify with others in their suffering (Isaiah 63:9; 2 Corinthians 1:4). Think about one way you have suffered. When you needed to talk to someone desperately about it, did you want to ask someone who had not been through the very same thing? Probably not. Why? Because they wouldn't understand since they couldn't relate. Being able to identify with someone's pain, to know what they're going through personally, is powerful.

Secondly, what we have suffered, if we let God use it, shapes us (Hebrews 12:5–11; 1 Peter 1:6–7). I wish we lived near a factory where they fashioned gold so that we could watch this verse unfold in real time. A lot in our lives hangs on us like the seaweed dredge that sticks to our bodies when we walk back onto shore from the ocean. We try to shake it off, but removing it isn't easy.

I'll mention a third reason. Suffering, painfully, reminds us not to get too comfortable because this—everything you see around you—is not home. Home is a beautiful, indescribable place that will take our breath away, full of love and life and adventure! Just trying to imagine our true home in this moment makes my heart race with excitement.

Is God always good? How could a good God then allow us to suffer, sometimes even vile and terrible miseries? The most important thing to remember about suffering is this: God did not put us through anything that God was not willing to also bear. God suffered more than anyone (Psalm 22; Matthew 27:46). Even now, since that cross event sent shockwaves through history, God continues to identify with us in our pain and pleads for us (Isaiah 63:9; Romans 8:34; Hebrews 7:25). God in human form suffered for us; God in Spirit comforts us in our suffering (John 14:26).

I believed a fancy little lie for most of my life, perhaps because of the easy comforts I had living in the U.S. The truth I discovered is this: you cannot live through life unscathed. So, don't think that because you are a Christian, you won't suffer. Sometimes when you are a Christian, it gets worse. Life does get better but not necessarily in some of the ways you might think or wish. God does not promise that we will be saved from the very same pains that touch everyone else: loss of income, sickness, injustice, death. Life shouldn't be this way, actually. That's why Christ seeks to bring us life again (John 10:10). So, in this in-between-time, the pain we endure has a purpose if we offer it to God.

Join the fellowship of his suffering,

Jenny

P.S.
Yes, that was my nod to *The Lord of the Rings*.

What Do You Believe?

1. How are you hurting right now?

2. How is God using, or how will God use, suffering for your good?

3. One of the best avenues to cope with suffering is to look beyond our own pain and aid others. Who is hurting that you can offer to help today?

Notes:

24

Vulnerability

The unclenched fist is still the best.
                                    – "All That is Gold" by Brooks Williams

Dear Open-handed,

Jesus lived vulnerably, not just in his way of life, but in his attitude of heart. Vulnerability does not mean weakness, although it can be mistaken as such. Vulnerability means living in the manner of Christ. This does not mean we necessarily let ourselves be taken advantage of. Being vulnerable does not mean being stupid and not protecting yourself at times, but it does mean being willing to endure injury far more than we would like. Choosing to be vulnerable displays a certain strength.

Scripture describes Jesus as both a lion and a lamb—the Lion of Judah, a strong, fierce, not-to-be-messed-with king of all animals and the Lamb of Calvary, a defenseless, meek, animal of weakness (Revelation 5:5–6; 7:10). I find these extremes fascinating. Jesus Christ will return to judge as the most awe-inspiring, fearful One to right all of the wrongs ever done. He returns as a warrior on a white steed but watch how Christ enters the world—as a helpless babe (Revelation 19:11–15). Why? How should we act once we have given our lives to follow Him? Read these verses that speak of Christ's vulnerability.

- Isaiah 53:7
- Philippians 2:5–8

These verses show us God decided that making God's own self vulnerable to humanity(!) was the very best way to demonstrate love, to win our hearts and our salvation. Vulnerability is powerful. Demonstrating it does not mean that others will necessarily respond, but if they do not, they are heaping judgment upon themselves.

In life, we often cut each other down, compensating from our own sense of deep pain, injury, and selfishness. To show vulnerability, at times, would be to invite injury, so I wouldn't do it unnecessarily. When to be vulnerable depends on the situation.

In being vulnerable, we forgo our right to fight back. Not that we can't defend ourselves, but Christ was mistreated and chose not to find back. Why? He of all people, the most innocent, did not fight back in a way that injured. He fought in a new way, a way that the world does not understand. In a given situation, we decide not to engage in the way the world fights. This can be silence, avoidance, and response, but not weakness. Jesus expects us to be innocent *and* shrewd (Matthew 10:16). Most people, myself included, are not asking God's Spirit how to be clever; our default is usually just to react defensively like anybody else would.

Like Christ, we do not apologize for being peaceable and holy. Usually, we're tripping over ourselves, falling so easily into imitating the world and participating in sin that we aren't being vulnerable at all. We are being selfish, judgmental, and retaliatory. Developing vulnerability takes time, wisdom, and confession. These verses demonstrate the vulnerability to what our Lord is calling us:

- Romans 12:10, 14, 17–20
- Luke 6:29
- 1 Thessalonians 5:4–9, 15

A scene in the movie *The Green Mile* demonstrates vulnerability in a huge, brawny man named John Coffey. He is mistreated and accepts these injuries, but he determines to protect others and not transfer his injuries to anyone else. This is a beautiful picture for the Christian; we protect others by being vulnerable ourselves.

Also, God remembers each injury we endure. God in justice will penalize all who do harm, and it is for them that we should pray—that God would forgive them, that God would have mercy on them—because God's wrath on a person is what no one can endure. At the end of time, God's judgment will be swift, sure, and unchangeable.

Demonstrating vulnerability now is the way that we testify to how Christ has changed us. It offers an opportunity to others, who are still in their sins, to accept a vulnerable Savior who willingly took on injury so they could be spared.

You are a precious jewel,

Jenny

What Do You Believe?

1. What does God want to show us through his wounds?

2. With whom should you be vulnerable? Why?

3. How and where do you draw the lines of trust, vulnerability, and unnecessary exposure to risk with someone?

Notes:

25

Life in Death

Dear Resurrected,

You've made great strides in following Christ, and what is more, you love him. You want God, and you don't want anything to get in the way of that.

> For to me, to live is Christ, to die is gain. (Galatians 2:20)

What in the world did Paul mean when he wrote that?

Perhaps this is the strangest contradiction of all. Our new life in Christ, when we become Christians, is the death of our old self. Who we were on our own (before we asked God to change us) died. One little proof that you really have become a child of God is when you sense, rapidly or slowly, that you have begun to have a greater desire to abandon temptation in order to obey God, that you have begun to want God more than anything else you used to love. The lures, which baited you so easily before, take a bit longer now to hook you.

A German single fellow executed by the Nazis at age 39, Dietrich Bonhoeffer, has perhaps offered the best explanation. He was a Christian living in Germany during World War II and made some very hard decisions as his country turned toward Hitler. I leave you with this very thick quotation. It's a lot to digest, I know! But it will be food for thought for years to come.

> Only in the cross and resurrection of Jesus Christ has death been drawn into God's power, and it must now serve God's own aims. It is not some fatalistic surrender, but rather a living faith in Jesus Christ, who died and rose for us, that is able to cope profoundly with death. In life with Jesus Christ, death as a general fate approaching us from without is confronted by death from within, one's own death, the free death of daily dying with Jesus Christ. Those who live with Christ die daily to their own will. Christ in us gives us over to death so that he can live within us. Thus our inner dying grows to meet that death from without. Christians receive their own death in this way, and in this way, our physical death very truly becomes not the end, but rather the fulfillment of our life in Jesus Christ. Here we enter into community with the one who at his own death was able to say, "It is finished."[22]

The symbol of dying daily, putting to death our desires—not that we are denying we have those desires, but that we are willing to sacrifice them for God—is our path to life! Take pride, for example. Heather Kopp shares about "the emptying of my ego. It's freeing to know that no one can hurt your pride because it's gone ... [I'm] daily relying on His power [to live]."[23]

Be fully alive,

Jenny

What Do You Believe?

1. Looking back, what is easier to give over to God (to kill) now than before?

2. What are you struggling to die to today?

3. What is so hard about giving that to God?

Notes:

Part Three:

Habits of a Christian

26

Forming Habits

Dear Disciple of Jesus,

Living as a Christian is a way of life, a way of being. Parents teach their children, for example, how to function in daily life (e.g. manners, tasks, potty training, etc.). In the same way, God has entrusted rituals to us to practice as spiritual children. This training forms us. Becoming a disciple of Christ means patterning your life after his and living his life in morality, in holiness, in love. He had some habits that helped him to build the patterns that God wants in us.

These rituals are habits that shape you emotionally, physically, and spiritually. These practices over time help to change your brain patterns, the thoughts and/or lies that are anti-God, and your approach to situations. These have been termed spiritual disciplines; I prefer to call them Christian habits.

How often should you practice these habits? God doesn't name a rigid number of times per day or week. We should do them as Christ did: intentionally, routinely, consistently. Much like playing a piano, the more you practice, the better you become. These Christian habits are exercises that help to strengthen you to live like Christ. Multiple lists have been compiled over the years, but generally include these exercises: prayer, confession, fasting, study, solitude, simplicity, joining, giving, relaxing, and serving.

I love the verses that Peter penned in 2 Peter 1:5–9:

> For this very reason [read the earlier verses to understand what follows and why], make every effort to add to your faith goodness; and to your goodness, knowledge; and to knowledge, self-control; and to self-control, perseverance, and to perseverance, godliness; and to godliness, brotherly kindness; and to brotherly kindness, love. For if you possess these qualities in increasing measure, they will keep you from being ineffective and unproductive in your knowledge of your Lord Jesus Christ. But if anyone does not have them, he is nearsighted and blind and has forgotten that he has been cleansed from his past sins.

These Christian habits, or exercises, *form* you. So if you want to be changed, practice! These practices help to perfect us, shaping us to Christ's form.

Practice makes perfect (Matthew 5:48),

Jenny

What Do You Believe?

1. Why do you think God gave us certain habits and exercises to practice?

2. From the list I mentioned above, which one(s) are you least familiar with?

3. What do you think practicing these habits will do for you?

Notes:

27

Listening to and Talking with God: Prayer

Dear Child of the Promise,[24]

"When we pray, we seek an opportunity to obey God."[25]

Prayer comes easier to some, so do not be discouraged if you do not feel successful. Prayer is about participation, not performance (Matthew 6:5–8). The point is to do it and repeat, and in so doing, you will form a habit of prayer. Remember that each spiritual habit exercises us spiritually, so the act of prayer actually changes us.

Think of prayer as a two-way conversation with God, an open line of communication. Quiet yourself before God, and pour your heart out. Slow down and think about how you're hiding from God. Like any communication, prayer involves listening, and the best way to hear God's voice is to read what God has said in Scripture. Often, prayer is a posture of waiting. Here is a good place to start and end every day:

> Dear God, you know me. I trust you. You know my original design before sin got in the way, and now I am messed up. Who did You make me to be? I want to be remade. Help me in this situation/circumstance/relationship . . .

I think of prayer as breathing, exhaling my junk from the day and inhaling God's great grace, love, mercy, hope, peace, provision, goodness, and wisdom—all the wonderful things God *wants* to give us, if we would only ask! Prayer is about remembering, recalling who God is and what God has done. I was taught the acronym ACTS:

Adoration:	Praising God
Confession:	Admitting our wrongs
Thanksgiving:	Thanking God
Supplication:	Asking God

Here is my breakdown. Prayer is remembering:

Who God Is
What God Wants
Who We Are
What God Has Done
What We Need

Either of these follow a pattern of praise and confession that many of us skip before we start petitioning God for all we think we want. If our prayers consisted of equal parts of each, our requests would then fill only 25% of our time in prayer. An exact formula for prayer is not the point; it is about righting our attitudes, emotions, and behaviors before the God of the universe and praying for the Kingdom of God to come.

We could do no better than to follow Christ's example in prayer, how he told us to pray. Consider the Lord's prayer in Matthew 6:9–13:

Our Father	Who God Is
who is in Heaven,	
Hallowed be your name,	
Your kingdom come,	What God Wants
Your will be done,	
On earth as it is in heaven.	
Give us this day	What We Need
our daily bread.	
Forgive us our debts,	Who We Are
As we forgive our debtors.	What God Wants
Lead us not into temptation,	
But deliver us from evil.	What We Need

One side comment. I've heard many quote Mark 11:24: "Therefore I tell you, whatever you ask for in prayer, believe that you have received it, and it will be yours." Jesus speaks this wonderful promise, and that's why we need to read every verse in its context to consider the whole testimony of Scripture together. How many claim verse 24 for themselves but overlook the very next thing Jesus says in verse 25? "And when you stand praying, if you hold anything against anyone, forgive him, so that your Father in heaven may forgive you your sins." How many of us are doing *this* in order to have our sins forgiven and our prayers answered?

Following Jesus, pray privately and pray together with other believers. The Christian life is not to be lived alone.

Breathe deeply,

Jenny

What Do You Believe?

1. What Do You Believe prayer does?

2. What makes it hard for you to pray?

3. What are you doing that might keep your prayers from being answered?

Notes:

28

Being Honest: Confession

Dear Candid,

Confession is also like breathing, exhaling the rubbish in our hearts and inhaling God's forgiveness. We need to do it daily. How and to whom? Confession, of course, can be done in a variety of ways—silently, verbally, written—but all are based in word. Pouring out our spirit to the One who needs to receive it.

Confession can mean a declaration of our beliefs but here refers to the naming of our sins. Confessing what we have done wrong or what we have failed to do is vital to keep our hearts pure, our minds clear, our spirits fresh.[26] You know how you sweat during a good run or hike? Impurities are released out of the body in exercising. Confessing our sins benefits us physically and spiritually because we are practicing a similar process of cleansing.

Confession, mind you, is not what cleanses us; Jesus's blood payment does that. We have to be honest with ourselves, however, in order to ask and receive what Jesus has done for us. I believe Scripture teaches us clearly that the only priest to whom we need to confess is Jesus Christ, the ultimate priest (Hebrews 4:14–5:10; 8:1–2). We do not need a third party between us and God to save us other than Jesus, who is God.

Think of those planks we hold in aerobics class. You know where we try to hold our bodies straight in alignment? Confession realigns us to God. Confession is a habit we must practice privately and together with other believers. Our words of confession are a form of worship (meaning acknowledging rightly who God is and who we are). In confession, we practice speaking the truth, reminding ourselves who God is, what God deserves, and that we do not have it all together. We blow it in some way or another often enough to need to practice the habit of confession daily.

Confession brings forgiveness and a good shower, so to speak (1 John 1:9). Confessing our sins is done most often to God, but we are to confess our sins also to one another (James 5:16). Why? Perhaps because we tend to think we are better than we are. Confessing a sin that I have committed against another is extremely humbling. Being reminded of how often we fall short is a good thing. Moreover, confession is the practice of being honest. It may seem easier to hide or avoid but that leads to being trapped, being held by something you did that you cannot tell anyone. Some sins you only need to confess to God; for other sins, you need to go to the person you hurt and acknowledge it openly. Whatever you did was wrong, and they deserve an apology.

I remember one time I had to confess to someone in college. It was humiliating, which motivated me to not sin again in that way to avoid the need for future confession! I had lied to my professor's teaching assistant about something (what I cannot recall, another good reason to confess sooner than later). I was so convicted about it that I made myself walk into his office and explain to him what I had done, come what may. He would not have known if I hadn't told him, but then again, I was cheating him out of the opportunity to do his job well. Christians cannot afford to live dishonestly (1 John 1:8, 10). Not confessing our wrongs cheats us out of being close to God. Confession reminds us to live in God's reality rather than in our private, skewed little fiefdom where the universe revolves around you-know-who. Keeping our list of unconfessed sins very short brings us good (Proverbs 28:13). Apart from the fact that we should confess, why would we *not* confess and cheat ourselves of its benefits?

With love,

Jenny

What Do You Believe?

1. What makes it difficult to confess your sins?

2. Read Genesis 3:8–10, Romans 8:1–2, and 1 John 3:1–3, 19–20. Do you struggle with still feeling ashamed after you've confessed your sins and turned from them? Why do you think this is?

3. What times of day this week will you set aside to confess your sins to God?

Notes:

29

Letting Go: Fasting

Dear Faithful,

Fasting, which is not eating for a sustained period, has been a Jewish and Christian practice for centuries. What does it accomplish? Well, similar to an athlete training for a race who has a programmed regime, fasting allows you grow as a Christian. Fasting will teach you things that you didn't know about yourself or God. Fasting teaches us how to suffer joyfully. Fasting is an act of humility, worship, and commitment (Psalm 35:13; Acts 13:2; 14:23). Fasting, above all, is done for a spiritual reason: to honor God as an act of obedience and to prepare ourselves for a purpose.

We teach ourselves quite naturally to run after whatever it is that we want. In fasting, we realize that we can decline basic physical survival instincts that scream at us. This particular exercise allows us to practice denying food and/or other things we could have but give up. Romans 16:18, Philippians 3:19, and 1 Corinthians 6:13 contrast how Christians should be able to refrain from self-indulgence. Fasting reminds us how to let go of what we want. What then should replace our mealtimes? Concentrated times of prayer and solitude are the most common to fill the would-be breakfast, lunch, and dinner.

Like the other exercises, fasting should be done routinely and purposefully. Jesus gives us directions on how to fast in Matthew 6:16–18 and Mark 2:18–19. Several have created quite sensible fasting plans (the Daniel fast, Miles McPherson's charts, etc.), and I'll leave you to google those. I'll only mention that fasting usually includes drinking only water for a time. Some fast one meal, one day, one week, or even forty days. The longer you fast, the more you need to add essential nutrients in some way (e.g. drinking fortified juices) and consult a dietician or doctor. You might also consider spending a week refraining from processed sugar and/or caffeine to prepare your body before you cut out food.

In fasting, we learn that food does not ultimately sustain us; God does. Fasting reminds us of our absolute dependence on God, and in our time without food, we experience how to live on bread—the word of God—alone (Matthew 4:4; John 4:32–34).

Love,

Jenny

What Do You Believe?

1. What can fasting teach us?

2. What does temporarily declining your physical desires
    have to do with living like a Christian?

3. Are there other reasons to fast? Hint: Esther 4:12–16;
    Matthew 9:15; Acts 13:2–3.

Notes:

30

Exploring: Study

Dear Daughter of the Book,

The indescribable God who created you loves you very much. We need daily reminders that God is for us. Tossed by the waves of trouble that come our way, we quickly lose sight of that. We are tempted to sink into doubt, which, if we're not careful, can lead to despair. Hopelessness is the opposite of what God has given to us. Where do we find hope?

Hope comes when you stop what you are doing and spend time with God. This time can be in prayer or observing nature or listening to music, but one of the best ways to hear God is to read what God has already said in the Bible. God breathed the words to be recorded (2 Timothy 3:16). If some chap mysteriously wrote you a love letter, wouldn't you be curious to read it? Some have called the Bible God's love letter to humanity. I'm not sure that's the best description, but it is a striking image. The Bible is historical; it is personal; it is easy to read; it is hard to read. It was written over 1500 years of history, so this is no ordinary book. Reading takes effort, but a reward is promised to its readers (Isaiah 55:11; Psalm 1:1–2; Psalm 119; Revelation 1:3).

For centuries, people were not encouraged to read the Bible by the larger church establishment. Some simply couldn't read at all, couldn't read the language in which the Bible was written, and/or they weren't taught to even consider reading it. Once the Bible was printed on a press in 1455 (allowing mass copies) and Martin Luther translated it into German by 1534 (allowing folks who couldn't read Latin to read the Bible), the situation began to change; however, in the 21st century, we may have swung to the other extreme. Reading the Bible individually is a great idea, but it's not like we can just read the Bible by ourselves and that be *enough*. We are to read the Bible with others. We are to listen to those who have studied the Bible longer and received more training in how to read the Bible. We can't live the Christian life or read the Bible in isolation.

The best way to love God is do what God has said to do (1 John 5:2–3). This means we have to learn God's Word. How are we to do that? Well, in lots of ways. Here are some ideas:

Reading

Read 3–5 chapters a day, or plan to read the Bible in two years.

Listening

Listen to the Bible read aloud or dramatized. This allows you to take in greater chunks of Scripture in one sitting. Since it is one grand story, sometimes reading individual chapters chops it up too much. This may be a great option for those with long work commutes. I recommend Max McLean's audio recording.

Studying

Follow a written outline for study, individually and in a group. Most anything by Kay Arthur or NavPress will serve you well.

Meditate

Read a few verses or a section, and chew on it for an extended period. What does it mean? What does it mean in my life today?

Memorize

I still remember the verses my mum gave me to memorize from my childhood. These Scriptures are recalled again and again in a time of need. You can create an index card file of verses or sticky-notes posted on your bathroom mirror. I like learning one a week, basically 50 in a year, and using the last two weeks to review those I've learned.

Share

Nothing teaches you like you having to teach the material to someone else, right?

Share bits and pieces of what you're learning to your friends and family members. Serve in your church's children program, for example.

Eat the Word of God daily to live (Matthew 4:4),

Jenny

What Do You Believe?

1. Where is your favorite place to read the Bible?

2. What are different ways to study and learn the Word of God (Bible)?

3. Why should your study of the Bible not *only* be by yourself?

Notes:

31

Stealing Away: Solitude and Silence

Dear Pilgrim,

As I write you this quiet morning, I find myself frustrated. Not at you, of course. The year's end marks several accounting items that I have addressed, but because other people have delayed doing their part, several things are not yet resolved. The "worries of this life" (Luke 12:22–32) are distracting my thoughts, and I'm tempted to surrender joy, a Christian's happy companion. So I smiled as I sat down and saw the next topic slated for me to write today.

You well know the craze of our lives. We are swept up in the rush and panic of daily drama. Christians over the centuries, mimicking Christ's example, have learned ways to pull away (Mark 6:31–32, 45–46). It takes energy and intention, but seeking times of solitude and silence as a spiritual exercise renews us. Slipping away from the din of the voices demanding our attention restores us. Slowing down, seeking God, being silent refreshes us in unique ways. Some people separate solitude and silence as different exercises, and they are. I pair them because as two perfect companions, they lead us to stillness together.

Seeking solitude, I plan periodic weekends or Saturdays to be spent alone every year. You may decide that one hour in the morning three times a week before everyone else wakes up is the best option possible in your current season of life. Be creative. Be consistent. Parks, creek banks, closets, cars, chapels, open fields, and bedrooms have all been quiet places that have worked for me. I've had friends loan me their vacant home for a day. I've stayed at a bed and breakfast, a monastery, and at home. God leaves it to us to determine how and how often to seek solitude, and you will know when you especially need to do it. Feeling overwhelmed is a good tip that it's time to steal yourself away. These are times to be still. Psalm 46:10a is a favorite of some to quote: "Be still, and know that I am God." But what's the second half of that verse? "I will be exalted among the nations. I will be exalted in the earth." Being still is *so that* we remember our place and God's and what God wants to do for the world. Solitude teaches us perspective, something we can't get any other way other than stopping and being alone with God. It's magnificent. Like any exercise, it takes some practice to get into it. You may find it awkward or difficult at first, but you'll get there.

How in the world does one practice silence? Lots of ways! Be speechless for a certain amount of time. Or watch what words you say in a given day. I'll not soon forget what my Haitian friend, who had come to study in the U.S., shared with me one day in class. He was shocked at how often he heard Americans, even professors, use the words I, me, and mine. His experience in Haiti was the opposite. Politeness, respect, and good living in Haiti means focusing more on others than oneself. Words like you and yours peppered their speech much more often than self-centered pronouns. I determined that day that one of the ways I would exercise silence was to spend certain days trying not to use personal pronouns. Try it. It's hilarious how hard it is.

God has given us such great imaginations, so I look forward to your ideas of how we can live in solitude and silence imitating the way of Christ.

Seek the quiet places and ancient paths (Jeremiah 6:16),

Jenny

What Do You Believe?

1. What does sitting still and being silent teach us?

2. Read Proverbs 10:19. From this verse, what is another reason for practicing silence?

3. Getting away is a practice, a habit, a discipline like anything else. How will you make this happen for you?

Notes:

32

Unfussing: Simplicity

Dear Imitator of God,[27]

Can you think of anyone who prefers to sit in bumper to bumper traffic? How about someone who thrives on shopping with insane crowds on Black Friday? Who wouldn't rather drive or shop when the pathways are clear? Perhaps that is how we should think of our lives. Keeping our lives from spiritual and physical clutter opens us to God in new ways. This is not to say that "cleanliness is next to godliness," and people vary in what they consider clutter. The point is that simplifying our lives is a spiritual exercise that we should be practicing routinely.

I call this simpling. You know my habit of coining new words, and simplicizing won't do. Simplifying is ok, but simpling—why not? Simpling is not just about going through our closets to make a run to Goodwill, although it includes that. It is a way of life. De-cluttering our minds to make every one of our thoughts obey Christ is priority (2 Corinthians 10:5). This is not an emptying of our minds as some Eastern philosophies teach; it is to take each thought and make it God's, good and life-giving.

De-cluttering extends to how we spend our time and money. At least annually, my husband and I take a half-day to think through how we spend the weeks and money God gives to us, asking what to add or subtract. With jobs, kids, deadlines, bills, and daily drama, most people run on auto-pilot, but with the craze that life brings we have to manually take the controls once in a while to rewrite the auto-pilot program.

If we live in the U.S., most of us have a lot of stuff. There's nothing necessarily wrong with that. The question is, how are we using what we have? Have we boarded the I-can't-get-rid-of-it-because-I-might-use-it-eventually train? Or take the size of your home. My husband and I lived in a 600 sq. ft. apartment for ten years, and we often were asked, "How do you live in that box?" Most of the world's population, in fact, live in apartments, flats, huts, etc., with three generations of some families sharing one room entirely. It's a matter of perspective, and simplifying helps us to see what God wants us to keep or give. Life is not found in wealth (Proverbs 11:28; Luke 12:15; 1 Timothy 6:9). Exercising our simpling muscles helps us to find the kingdom of God (Matthew 6:33; 13:45–46; 19:16–22).

What if we started asking ourselves if we should downsize in order to pay down debt or perhaps move into a larger place to provide for someone who might need to live with us? Simpling is an art that everyone needs to practice. It opens ways for God to bless us. We tend to consume without question, but how much do we need? Slow down, and answer these questions:

- How could you simplify your schedule?
- How can something you have be used to bless someone else?
- What thoughts plague you?

- Assuming you sleep eight hours a night, how might you spend the remaining 112 hours in a week differently?
- How many pairs of shoes do you need?
- What does Jesus call a hoarder (Luke 12:16–21)?
- What has God asked you to give away?
- Whom do you need to forgive?
- In what areas have you succumbed to the fancy little idea that bigger-and-newer-is-always-better?
- In what areas of your life has having too much clouded good judgment?

With affection,

Jenny

What Do You Believe?

1. Simplicity extends to how you spend the money you are given. How could you be smarter with money?

2. Richard Foster lists ten suggestions for simplicity that I rephrase here.[28]

   1. Buy useful things not trophy things.
   2. Refuse what you're becoming addicted to.
   3. Every day, give away.
   4. Don't be seduced by advertisements. (Bigger, faster, sweeter, etc. isn't always better.)
   5. Enjoy things without having to own them.
   6. Explore nature.
   7. What will "Buy now, pay later" cost you?
   8. Say what you mean and will do (Matthew 5:37).
   9. Refuse what oppresses others.
   10. Turn from whatever distracts you from pursuing God and his kingdom (Matthew 6:33).

3. Which of those listed above have you aced and which of those do you need to improve?

Notes:

33

Joining: Church

Dear Member of Christ's Body,

Remember the disabled guy who wanted to meet Jesus? The story is recounted in Luke 5:17–26. He wanted to be healed, and he needed his four friends to do it. Because of his physical limitation, he couldn't get from Jesus what he needed without depending on others. That is a great picture of why each of us needs a local church; we need others to grow spiritually.

In the U.S., I regularly hear, "Oh, I don't need to go to church. I pray and talk to God on my own." *What?* God created the church for us to be a part of it, to be together. Check out Acts 2:42–46; 1 Corinthians 12:12–13, 27; Hebrews 10:25. The Christian life is not one lived in isolation. God, remember, as the Trinity, is all about relationships!

God created the church for lots of great reasons, but I'll mention only two: worship and interdependence. God wants us to worship together. There's something good to God and for us to worship as a group. We experience God in new ways as we worship together; we are changed in ways different than when we worship alone.

Depending on others to guide you in your spiritual walk will also guard against self-delusion. Why? Because we are forgetful and we are easily deceived. We think too much of ourselves if we think we can make it alone as a

Christian. That was never God's design. Even though we have been redeemed and are being remade, we still have the ability to turn from God in any choice we make. We need others to help us see our wrongs. We "use our connection to other Christians as the vehicle *by which* Christ ministers life to us."[29]

I love how Levi Lusko compares Christians to lions and describes the protection we receive in joining a local church.

> Lions are the only truly social cat; their strength comes not from the individual but from the whole pride. That's why the author of Hebrews warned Christians to not fall into the bad habit of missing church (Hebrews 10:25). Satan wants us separated from the pride so we are easier to pick off.[30]

Whether we are tender seedlings fresh in our faith or solid oak trees with deep roots of faith, something about being together—hearing God's word, worshipping, and serving together—nurtures us in a way unlike anything else. It takes works and energy, and doing your own thing will always seem easier, but *whose* life are we living? Church is full of broken people, and even still, God means for us to go there to grow.

Protect your pack,

Jenny

What Do You Believe?

1. What reasons have you heard from people about why they don't go to church?

2. Are the reasons people give for not going to church valid? Why or why not?

3. Why do you go to church?

Notes:

34

Giving: Tithe

Dear Giver,

Another important habit for a Christian is giving, sharing a portion of whatever you have with others. Giving flows from a heart of generosity. As I have already written, give of your time, talents, resources, story, and your spirit. Share with others whatever God has given you.

Tithing refers to one kind of giving: monetary. Tithing is offering to God through the church a proportion of the money we have been given to share. It's a discipline like anything else and takes practice. It is an act of worshipping God. We may differ on what amount, but all should give, regularly and generously. It won't happen unless you intentionally set up a plan to give.

As Christians, we believe "our" money is actually God's money. God guides us how to spend it. Think of handling money as one would sheep—as a shepherd, a steward. We've lost that sense as cultures have industrialized, but the responsibility given to humanity in Genesis was to care for the earth. As Christians, we are stewards to tend those around us, using the money we have been given to bring greater good to our community. Instead of thinking in terms of "How much must I give?" ask yourself, "How much should I keep?"

Woody Glenn, an attorney in Dallas and an esteemed friend of ours, once described the attitudes that Christians may have in giving money back to God through the church.[31] The first attitude is one of guilt, people give because they feel guilty. The next attitude is perhaps a step up. People feel a duty, a forced obligation to give. Folks would rather not give but feel like they have to give. That's something, but I wonder if God enjoys that about as much as a wife would enjoy a husband giving her an anniversary gift out of obligation. Another attitude, a step even closer perhaps, is that people give out of obedience. They give because they want to obey God, and that's good. They know it's right and a good thing to do, so they muscle through it, not from a sense of being forced but still without joy. The attitude God wants us to have, however, is to give from gratitude and joy. God wants us to give openly, freely, cheerfully, sacrificially. God doesn't need it, but we really need to give it—because of what giving does for us, in us. This fourth perspective is how we should give.

Is a certain percentage required? That's not the right question. The Jewish law outlined rules of tithing, which may have made it easier in being defined, but Jesus expanded this beyond a set percentage. It's much harder to wrestle through one's motivations and determine how much one should give freely out of love.

Money is a tool, but the "love of money" ensnares both the rich and the poor (1 Timothy 6:10). Those poorer daydream about becoming rich, spending what little money they have unwisely. Others who are rich are consumed in not losing their wealth. Of course, few desire poverty, but contentment and true wealth have little to do with money.

What if you haven't been taught about how to use money? Many of us missed the boat on how to budget, how to use money wisely, how to save, how to make good financial choices. If you have this deficit (pun intended), find another Christian wiser in this area to teach you. Our parents can't cover everything, but God fills those gaps through people in your church. We're a family, remember.

Being able to give financially means being good with money in general. Ron Blue offers five principles that will serve you well.

1. Spend less than you earn.
2. Avoid debt.
3. Keep a cushion ($ for emergencies that you don't touch).
4. Save a portion each month for the future.
5. Give generously.

Here's a wee bit of our story. As newlyweds in 2003, my husband and I stared into the face of our future with substantial student loans. Neither of us came from wealth, so we learned a crucial lesson: live on less and save like crazy. We gave a portion of our income every week to God no matter what (starting small and increasing as a percentage of our income over the years). We paid off those loans in full, three years later. We have freedom to make decisions without the burden of debt. My husband was able to actually consider and apply for pastoral positions, which we would have avoided altogether if we had had to pick based on how much they paid in order to keep up with loan payments. Trust God with your money and give!

May your heart shine from the gifts you have shared,

Jenny

What Do You Believe?

1. What are you currently sharing with your local church? List everything.

2. What are you currently financially giving to your local church and other ministries?

3. Does giving that amount bring you joy (2 Corinthians 9:6–7)? Should it be less? Should it be more?

Notes:

35

Relaxing: Shabbat

Dear Restful,

The main thing about our Christian faith is that we did not earn it. No amount of striving or suffering or doing anything could have made us clean before God. All the vain effort to try to do so is religion. God swooped down to save us and make it right. And now we can know God. Closely. Warmly. Personally.

We seem to understand that at salvation and then promptly forget. We try to live like Christians from our own strength and muscled effort. One of the best habits we can practice is to remind ourselves that our faith in God's work for us is the weekly tradition of relaxing! Playing! Resting! Not *having* to do anything in particular whatsoever. For those who like to stay busy, this is hard. But forcing ourselves to stop, unwind, slow down, and rest matters very much.

God rested on the seventh day of creation. God called the Jewish people to observe Shabbat, or Sabbath, the designated day of rest from Friday's sunset to Saturday evening. For one, God said to rest. Read Genesis 2:2–3; Exodus 20:8–11, 31:17, 34:21; Mark 2:23–27; Hebrews 4:8–9.

For two, we need it. Physically. Emotionally. Spiritually.

In our crazed culture, one has to intentionally decide to stop making money or finishing a checklist or running their kids everywhere. It takes not letting the day be swept away by constant digital demands.

Cease from work. That's the deal. Not just from the work at your job, but from any work that causes you to furrow your brow, to think too hard, to feel stress.

Instead of "be still," Psalm 46:10 is also translated "Cease striving . . ." How appropriate!

Check out Isaiah 30:15:

This is what the Sovereign LORD,
the Holy One of Israel, says:
"In repentance and rest is your salvation,
    in quietness and trust is your strength,
    but you would have none of it."

That is one of my favorite verses.

Jewish people still observe Shabbat from sundown Friday to sundown Saturday. Some pick Saturday or Sunday. Others pick their day based on their work schedule. Just pick one. The point is to have a portion of time set aside for rest. Where you cease striving. Where you do what you want to do for fun. Christians can get so serious that they are the worst at obeying God in this area! We shouldn't feel like we're racing around out of breath all the time. Something's off. Why do we have so much on our plate that we can't fit in what God requires of us?

Take a rest. Once a week. Repeat.

The habit of resting one day a week takes faith that everything else that needs doing will get done. It reminds us that God is in control, that we are not. It reminds us that

God wants good things for us, not just toil (Ecclesiastes 2:24–26; 5:18–20). This is one very important thing to learn and remember about God. God actually wants us to take it easy at times, to have fun! He gave it to us as a gift (Exodus 16:29). God is honored when he sees us enjoying ourselves, living in the hope of his grace and mercy and provision. Why are we denying him, and ourselves, that pleasure? Silly creatures!

Live it up,

Jenny

What Do You Believe?

1. Why do you think God created a day for relaxing?

2. Is it hard for you to slow down and stop? Why or why not?

3. What are your favorite ways to rest?

Notes:

36

Playing Your Part: Service

Dear Servant of God,

Lest you were misinformed, becoming a Christian is not about being freed to do whatever you want. We were freed from being superglued to evil and death to become enslaved to a new master. It's another paradox of the Christian faith: we were liberated to become servants of God (Luke 22:26–27; John 12:26; Romans 6:22).[32] We were freed to be able to choose to do good. Serving means putting others' needs before our own. It gives us a chance to show faith and confidence that God will take care of us. It means surrendering our rights to what we could have. Our humility is what God is after. When we are humble enough to realize that we don't actually deserve anything from God, that God doesn't owe us anything, humility frees us to give. If we understood what God has given us, what could we possibly hold back from others?

Serving others is giving your time, energy, things, and money—even, perhaps especially, in those times when you feel like you do not have much—to help others. Whether helping with children's church, scouring the church toilets, or redecorating the youth room, you show the love of Christ in many acts of service for God, and this not only by your deeds, but in your attitude of service. Some find it easier than others, and this may relate to whether God has spiritually gifted them. All of us, however, are called to serve (Mark 10:45). Michael Card's song, "Basin and Towel," beautifully depicts serving.

Serving others as a spiritual act of Christian worship comes in many forms, as you know. The key is to pick a local church, and serve regularly. For example, are you praying for your pastor and church leaders often? Some choose to serve in one or two specific ways consistently, which perhaps works for most, rather than a one-off event with months in between. Sometimes, we shouldn't choose how we'd like to serve; sometimes the church has specific needs, and we just need to volunteer. Also, when we think about what to do, some tasks require not just heart, but skill. Be ready to listen if others suggest where we might serve and where we should not. Our egos should not be bruised because we've left our egos at the cross, crucified along with all of our sins. The life we live is Christ's. He never worried over what people thought of him, if he was impressing them, or which tasks were beneath him. He lived to do the will of our Father. What is God's will?

- Micah 6:8
- Isaiah 61:1–2 with Luke 4:17–21
- Matthew 28:18–20
- Luke 19:10
- James 1:27

Your motivation (that is, why are you serving whom you are serving?) is important to think through. Are we serving to get attention? Are we serving others to feel needed? Do we serve out of obligation? These are the attitudes God wants us to inspect and clean up so that our giving can be sincere. Have you signed up for too much? Why? Some avoid serving; some serve for the wrong reasons. And there are seasons of service. The Christian does not ever stop serving, but certain times may require you to pull back from tasks or step up in a greater way, depending on what's going on in your life. Sometimes that will require us to serve when and where we naturally would rather not. That is why it's like exercising. We don't always feel like doing it, but to be a healthy Christian, we do it anyway. But all of your hard work, if done honestly, is rewarded.

If you already love God, that's the number one thing in doing what God says (1 John 4:15–16; 5:3). You serve others out of your love for God. Your motivation, your heart, is to bless others as God has blessed you, to pass on what you have received, to pay it forward. It's beautiful and brings God great joy. Because you are a daughter of God and deeply loved, you are filled and spilling over with God's love to give (1 John 4:19). God—Father, Son, and Spirit—will show you how. At times, it will require what you are not inclined to give, but it will be worth it. I promise. Well, actually God promises (Mark 9:41; 1 Corinthians 3:13–14; 2 Corinthians 5:10).

Love well,

Jenny

What Do You Believe?

1. Why is sacrifice part of God's plan?

2. Which extreme do you tend toward: overserving or underserving? Why?

3. What does serving have to do with love?

Notes:

37

Summary of Habits:
Acts of Worship

Dear Worshipper of God,

All these habits are acts of worship to the one true God who deserves all our attention. I have described ten as a summary, not as a complete list. I do not separate them as individual acts or acts done together with others because some of these are done both ways. For example, you should pray (fast, serve, confess, etc.) by yourself and with others. Others describe them differently. Richard Foster breaks down spiritual habits this way:

Disciplines of Abstinence	*Disciplines of Engagement*
Solitude	Study
Silence	Worship
Fasting	Celebration
Frugality	Service
Chastity	Prayer
Secrecy	Fellowship
Sacrifice	Confession
	Submission

Dallas Willard lists them as:

The Inward Disciplines	*The Outward Disciplines*	*The Corporate Disciplines*
Meditation	Simplicity	Confession
Prayer	Solitude	Worship
Fasting	Submission	Guidance
Study	Service	Celebration

Love,

Jenny

Part Four:

Reading the Bible as a Christian

38

Why and How to Study God's Word

Dear Fellow Explorer,

There are, of course, many ways to study the Bible. Which method you use depends on your answer to this question. For what are you studying the Bible? Are you studying to gain insight and knowledge? Are you starting from a place of disbelief? As you read, are you demanding that God prove himself to you? Are you studying the Bible because you believe that it is the Word of God given to us through God's chosen authors? Knowing us, we have a mixture of motivations. And God loves us. God wants us to read the Bible irrespective of how we come to it, for who of us can come to it purely without our preconceived, stunted notions of who we think God is? God knows his Word has power to bring life to our hearts. So read!

Having said that, I do think it matters how you come to the text if you seek some benefit from it. Melissa Danisi makes some good points about this.[33] Why read the Bible? Because despite the vulnerability of language, despite the scribes' minor copy errors over the centuries, despite being penned by men (which is not necessarily a disadvantage), if God *is*, then God can preserve the words and their meaning that God intended. If God can do this, then this book is holy and sacred and meaningful and beautiful.

When reading the Bible, I suggest we read it because we believe God can speak to us through it. We come to the text needing to be changed, wanting to understand, and expecting to be transformed in our thinking, in our being, and in our behaving (Romans 12:1–2; 2 Timothy 3:16–17). Personal change comes by training, unlearning bad patterns and relearning better ways of thinking. Changing our thinking, changing our brain chemistry (literally and metaphorically), in turn, tunes our emotions and behavioral responses.

The ways you can study the Bible are numerous. Pick what best fits your current season of life.

- Are you a morning or evening person? Try reading one chapter a day either at the beginning or end of the day or on your lunch break.
- Do you commute long hours to work? Then listen to Max McLean read the Bible aloud. This allows you to hear greater chunks of God's Word in one sitting. Considering that so much of the Bible is written as a narrative (that is, a story), listening is a great option.
- Do you prefer a systematic regimen? Follow a plan for reading the Bible in one or two years.
- Wonder who wrote what when? Read the Chronological Bible that organizes the books in their sequence of events.
- Take shorter sections and reflect on each portion read. Journal your thoughts as you engage with the text and see if and how it relates to what is going on in your life at present.

Start with these basic questions when reading the Bible. Think about what the text is saying about who God is and how that impacts your life personally.

Looking:	What does the text say? What do you see?
Understanding:	What does it mean? What did the author mean for the original readers to understand?
Applying:	What does this passage show us about God's character? How does this passage relate to your life?

Mark Eckart creates an acronym LEAP,[34] and I've adapted it here:

Look into the text:	What does it say?
Examine the text:	What does the writer mean?
Add other verses:	What can other parts of the Bible teach us about it?
Practice:	How should I change as a result of studying it?

These six questions are another great guide to ask as you study the Scriptures.[35]

Does this text reveal something . . .

1. . . . I should believe about God?
2. . . . I should praise or thank or trust God for?
3. . . . I should pray about for myself or others?
4. . . . about which I should have a new attitude?
5. . . . about which I should make a decision?
6. . . . I should do for the sake of Christ, others, or myself?

The last and most important thing is that you study the Bible as a whole, repeatedly. Devotional guides are nice but leave out very important bits. Don't settle by just reading those in your time spent alone with God. As one of my friends, Dr. Sandi Glahn, shares, the downside of bite-sized devotional books is:

> (1) We don't know our Bibles; (2) we never learn the psalms; (3) we are left with the idea that the Bible is written directly to us (a self-focused Western approach) and that (4) it's a collection of motivational quotes rather than one grand story . . . and (5) we *end up worshiping a God who is all love and encouragement and never angry, holy, or willing to give people a good kick in the pants.*[36]

Your study buddy,

Jenny

What Do You Believe?

1. What Do You Believe about the Bible?

2. What do you think reading the Bible will do?

3. Why would God leave us a written message at all? Hint: Acts 17:25–26.

Notes:

39

God's Foundation: Books of the Law

Dear Wanderer,

God loves us so much, and perhaps because we would so often lose our way, God made sure the truth was written down. As we understand it, Moses recorded the first five books of the Bible: *Genesis, Exodus, Leviticus, Numbers*, and *Deuteronomy*. These five form the Pentateuch or the Torah, which the Jewish community also generally recognizes as God's Word. Remember in grade school when we had to find the topic sentence in each paragraph? Well, God, as any good writer, has a main point to each of these books in addition to recording history. Here are my sentence summaries:

Genesis: God begins the world and starts a family, but his children don't trust him.

Exodus: God is pure yet personally saves.

Leviticus: God explains the way back to God—through blood sacrifice.

Numbers: God requires faith and judges those who ignore God.

Deuteronomy: "Let's try this again, folks."

While these books primarily record God's history with Israel for the world (Exodus 6:7, 7:5; Leviticus 10:1–3), some principles are applicable to all who read these books. The Ten Commandments, originally given to the Jewish people (twice—once in Exodus and again in Deuteronomy), is an example. Remember, God's desire is to be with us; however, because God is pure goodness and we are stained by our sins, we offend God. Think about what it's like to be around a foul odor.

God communicated what it takes to be pure. Here is "God's Top Ten" of what an Israelite had to do to be a good person (Exodus 20:1–17; Deuteronomy 5:6–21):

#1 – Have no other gods except God.
#2 – Have no idols before God.
#3 – Don't misuse God's name.
#4 – Rest on day seven of the week.
#5 – Honor your mom and dad.
#6 – Don't murder.
#7 – Don't have sex with someone else's spouse.
#8 – Don't steal.
#9 – Don't lie about your neighbor.
#10 – Don't envy what is your neighbor's.

Yep, we have pretty much blown all of these, and once you're not good, no amount of adding "goodness" to your life résumé will make a difference (Matthew 5:20–22, 27–28; Romans 3:10, 20; James 2:10).

These rules were *gifts for life* from God to protect and teach the Hebrews, a new group God formed (Genesis 12:1–3; Deuteronomy 30:15–20). Just as a parent instructs their toddler how to behave with simple rules, mostly dos and don'ts, God was giving the basics to the children of Israel. Rules provide guidance and structure. Of course, they can be overdone, but not by God. God in supreme wisdom gifted us with guidelines to keep us safe. We won't understand all the rules, but we certainly can question and ponder them. God will explain more when we can handle it. Rules and restrictions are blessings toward life from a benevolent God.

Some may discard the Hebrew Scriptures as being archaic or replaced by the Greek New Testament. These Scriptures help us understand God's whole message! God's rules of conduct showed the Jewish people that they could never be good enough in their brokenness. God intended the law to teach them—and by extension, us—how far everyone falls short of God's goodness (Romans 3:19–20; Galatians 3:24). These books show us how miserably the Jewish people failed, as we also do on a daily basis, and point us to our desperate need to be saved by God from judgment!

The law covers several subject areas: dietary instructions, animal sacrifice, and morality, for example. Why do we practice certain parts now and not others? This is an important question and requires further study.[37] Briefly, God gave the Old Covenant intending to bring his children into the New Covenant (Ezekiel 11:19; 36:26; Jeremiah 31:33; Hebrews 8:10). Ethnic separation is no longer necessary; therefore, dietary instructions no longer apply (Acts 11:1–18; Romans 14:20). Morality laws were to lead people toward holiness (Matthew 19:4–6; Romans 1). Animal sacrifices for sins were necessary because of our inability to be holy; they are no longer necessary because of Jesus's full and final payment. All of the laws were fulfilled by Jesus Christ (Matthew 5:17–18). Christ's resurrection gives us the ability to behave morally (Ephesians 2:1–10).

Never stop marveling at the law and life God has given us,

Jenny

What Do You Believe?

1. Why did God give us directions in how to live?

2. When you don't do what you know that you're sup-
    posed to do, what do you feel? Why?

3. If you do the right thing for the wrong reason, what's
    wrong with that? Hint: Isaiah 29:13; Matthew 15:8–9.

Notes:

40

Never Forget: Historical Books

Dear Traveler,

I get it. Not everyone liked studying history in school. The funny thing about the human race is our collective amnesia. We forget what did not work before and repeat past mistakes. History reminds us, so we should study it. God knows how forgetful we are, and the historical books of the Bible record the events of God's first people. Amidst the multiple religious options of that day, God intended the Jewish people to showcase his holiness to the world and did not want them running after other gods (Genesis 15:13–14; 2 Kings 22:16–17). The Hebrews, also called the Israelites, grew into a distinct people, so much so that other nations considered them a political threat.

Twelve books comprise this historical section of the Bible: *Joshua, Judges, Ruth, 1* and *2 Samuel, 1* and *2 Kings, 1* and *2 Chronicles, Ezra, Nehemiah,* and *Esther.* The events of these books occur during the period 1400 to 500 B.C.[38] God has faithfully preserved the history of the Jewish people, their succession of kings, their political alliances and exploits, their successes and failures. This is no scrubbed history; the good, bad, ugly, and the very embarrassing are recorded.

What shines through these books is God's love and faithfulness to his people in the promises (covenants)[39] God made with them—despite Israel not holding up their end of the deal. This differentiates a contract (a business transaction where parties are released if the other defaults) from a covenant. Israel never approached God to form a covenant. Every time, God offered the covenant, and when Israel failed to meet the terms, God remained loyal to them. It's beautiful. God loves us so very much, and we know this by how God treated Israel over those centuries (with favor and discipline like any good parent). God is moving through history, despite our negligence, to offer us a way back.

Many struggle to believe that God would instruct Israel to destroy the surrounding nations when they moved into the region, Canaan. Previous generations have not struggled with this, but with our contemporary sentiment, we recoil. It looks vicious, like ethnic cleansing or genocide. Some explain it away by changing the events that occurred, by claiming the texts are inaccurate, or by claiming the God from those times is different from the God in Jesus. These are dangerous errors.

There is one God, and the God of the New Testament is the God of the Old. Some have charged God with committing genocide in the Old Testament (this is impossible if God is only good). Others have responded rightly to these concerns.[40] Such wisdom! There is one God, who does not change (Malachi 3:6), and we must wrestle with the truth. Church leadership has historically acknowledged these books as authentic. What if we took them at face value and gave God the benefit of the doubt in our doubt? What if we believed these records were true? What would that say about God? What do you think?

So far, I've come to this. God is revealed as Judge (Psalm 50:3–6; 75:7; Ecclesiastes 3:17; Romans 2:16).

People who think of Jesus as just a nice person or good prophet have not read enough of the Bible (2 Corinthians 5:10; Revelation 19:11–16). God's judgments are always good, not humanlike. Humans destroy from revenge or injustice; God destroys in perfect and pure justice. We all stand judged before God as evil perpetrators of violence and hatred (Matthew 5:21–22). God did not judge those nations to wipe out an ethnicity; God was judging evil. The purpose was clear: to teach everyone that the LORD is the one true God in all the world and to give them a chance to respond in faith (Romans 2:4–5). God did not play favorites with Israel either, looking the other way at their immorality (Numbers 16; 26:10; Romans 2:9–11). These warnings should disturb us. Our response to God should be to bow in respect and awe and confess our sins. God is serious about how we live (Hebrews 10:28–31).

May you not forget the part you play in God's story,

Jenny

What Do You Believe?

1. What can we learn from history?

2. What's the point of including genealogies in the Bible?

3. What is one mistake you fear repeating in your family?

Notes:

41

Crying Out to God: Books of Poetry and Wisdom

Dear Gem of God,

Whenever you question God's love for you, or the purpose of life, or why you are going through what you are, God's poetry will especially touch your heart. Moving from story form in the previous books, these books—*Job, Psalms, Proverbs, Ecclesiastes*, and *Song of Solomon*—are books of poetry and wisdom, songs of passion and despair, notes of expectation and promise. In fact, about one-third of the Bible is poetry.[41] Why do you think that would matter? Who do you imagine God to be? What kind of person? Which qualities does God have? What personality traits?

We might naturally imagine God with human-ish characteristics, but the order is the reverse. If humans are loving, they are reflecting something of the "image of God" that God has placed in us because God is love (1 Corinthians 13:4–8a; 1 John 4:8). God, perfect Love, outshines human attempts at love. God loves without prejudice, loyally, sacrificially. The poetry of God's Word illustrates God's heart with word pictures. Language falls short of describing God, so images add another representation of this-God-who-cannot-be-contained. These books portray in part who God is.

The events of *Job* happen during the time of Abraham (2000–1900 B.C.) most likely. I love the book of *Job* for raising the hard questions we all ask—the uneasy subjects of spiritual power, injustice, suffering, and evil. For most of the book, God lets a man in his anguish, Job, question God! This is remarkable! God does not scorch Job on the spot; God listens. So, God can handle you getting mad at Him. Be honest with where you are, and cry out to God! More amazingly, God, being God, bothers to *answer* Job. Mind blown. Before God is finished, Job is speechless and satisfied, but, interestingly, not because God had answered any of Job's questions (Job 40:5; 42:2–6). Job 11:13–19 are some of my favorite verses in the Bible. It's great advice by Zophar even though he gave it at the wrong time:

> Yet if you devote your heart to him
>> and stretch out your hands to him,
> if you put away the sin that is in your hand
>> and allow no evil to dwell in your tent,
> then, free of fault, you will lift up your face;
>> you will stand firm and without fear.
> You will surely forget your trouble,
>> recalling it only as waters gone by.
> Life will be brighter than noonday,
>> and darkness will become like morning.
> You will be secure, because there is hope;
>> you will look about you and take your rest in
>> safety.
> You will lie down, with no one to make you afraid,
>> and many will court your favor.

An iTunes playlist is how you might imagine *Psalms*, the book of 150 psalms. They are a Jewish collection of songs. I remember an African-American preacher in a television interview recommending that for anyone who doesn't feel God in the pain of life, they should read the psalms. These are gut-wrenching, emotional cries out to God, some from joy, some from grief. The psalms differ in expression: some call out the wonder of God, confession to God, gratitude to God, and lament to God. Wisdom psalms instruct (Psalm 1; 37; 119), and royal psalms herald God's reign as King and the future rule of God's Messiah (e.g. Psalm 2; 20; 47; 93; 96–99; 144). Just as Shakespeare followed a set of poetic rules, Hebrew poetry has a particular arrangement. More on that later.

Proverbs loosely falls in this arrangement as a book of wisdom. *Proverbs* is a collection of wise sayings to teach us how God wants us to live. For those of us who didn't have great fathers, your Father in heaven provides here the wisdom you wished you had been taught. These proverbs are principles for you, not God's personal promises to you, as my seminary professor, Dr. Ron Allen, first reminded me. *Ecclesiastes* is another book of wisdom, and it makes at least two brilliant points. First, this life is a mere breath, a vapor, a short-lived, uncertain, fragile existence. Lest we stop there depressed, the second point is to enjoy it, this same fleeting life! Whatever we are given, we are to honor God and make the most of it. The *Song of Solomon*, similar to a love letter, describes the beauty of marriage between a man and woman.

May you encounter more deeply this God of love and passion,

Jenny

What Do You Believe?

1. Think of a time when you were brutally honest with God. What did you learn about God in that experience?

2. What do emotions teach us about God?

3. What do you struggle to admit to God?

Notes:

42

God's Heart: Major Prophets

Dear Exile,

Prophets of God are a special group of folks, kind of like the guy who speaks on behalf of the president at a press conference. They are appointed by God to communicate an extremely important message, in the Old Testament, usually to:

1. Foretell something, like a very specific detail about the Messiah Savior or a coming war and/or

2. Call people out on their ridiculous sinning and warn people with their last chance to fall before God and beg forgiveness for their vile actions (such as neglecting those in need, faking their interest in God, getting rich on the backs of the poor, sexual immorality, abandoning the good ways of *YHWH*, the Hebrew word for God).

Being selected as a prophet is not glamorous. Isaiah gives his children awful names to forewarn God's judgment that was coming; Jeremiah is forbidden to marry; Hosea is told to marry a prostitute; Ezekiel cooked over human dung; John the Baptist ate locusts; Jesus wandered in the desert. God can ask any of us to do unfamiliar and unexpected things, but prophets are given special orders. God gives them very unique tasks for a specific purpose.

Balaam, Samuel, Nathan, Deborah, Samson, and others were also prophets, but they didn't write a separate book about it. The authors and books of the major prophets, called major for their length, are *Isaiah, Jeremiah, Lamentations* (likely written also by Jeremiah), *Ezekiel,* and *Daniel.* They describe God's huge heart of compassion for everyone. These books remind us how often God gave anyone and everyone a last chance, multiple times! God doesn't seem to have done anything (like bring judgment) without duly informing the Jewish people and the surrounding pagan nations in full disclosure. God is very repetitive in this regard, giving chance upon chance to people to come to terms with what his goodness requires. God will not stand for evil, meaning God is gracious and loving and merciful, but at the point he designates, God responds to our evil with judgment, as he should if God is a good God. How could a good God let evil continue?

These books record the events that teach us that God loves us very much, tries again and again to save us, and also means business. You'll read heartbreaking events that happen as the forewarned consequence for ignoring God. Think R-rated violence and worse. It's harsh, and some have a problem with God over it, but then again, how else is evil dealt with? God shows extravagant, constant love and kindness, sends multiple emissaries and diplomatic units (prophets), and still no response. Then what?

Here is a basic run-down for each of the books of the major prophets written during 750–500 B.C.:

Isaiah

Forecasting doom for the split kingdom of Judah and Israel and neighboring nations for their sins, Isaiah extends comfort and details about Jesus (check out Chapters 7–12 and 49–53).

Jeremiah

Jeremiah warns for forty years that Babylon will ransack Judah (which actually happens by 586 B.C.) and condemns nine other nations. The New Testament is not the first to mention the new plan (New Covenant) God brings; Jeremiah declares it in Chapter 31.

Lamentations

The fall of Jerusalem (in Judah) is recalled in crushing lament, and the anger and love and mercy of God are considered.

Ezekiel

Ezekiel (living with the Jewish exiles taken to Babylon) weeps over the judgment pronounced on Judah and seven surrounding nations, but foretells the reunification of Judah and Israel and a vision of a new land, temple, and city where God is. He also reveals the New Covenant coming (Ezekiel 34:25; 36).

Daniel

> A guy who stays true to God despite cultural opposi-
> tion, Daniel prophesies what God is going to do up to
> the end of time.

Sounds crazy, right? And if it wasn't from God, we
wouldn't believe it. Next to *Revelation*, I think these books
are some of the harder in the Bible to read. Prophetic messages are tricky to understand, so don't feel like you have
to or can figure everything out by yourself. That's why we
have church communities, pastors, and scholars who write
books about the Bible—to learn together. Many have written commentaries (composed of, literally, running
comments on each verse of a book or section of the Bible).
As you study further and are ready to dive deeper, I recommend starting with *The Bible Knowledge Commentary
Series* or Dr. Constable's Bible Study Notes (free and
online).[42]

Remember that God withholds his judgment as long as
possible,

What Do You Believe?

1. Why did God send prophets to people?

2. Read Isaiah 9:2–7 and 52:13–53:12. These verses are describing someone; who do these verses remind you of?

3. What do these verses (Lamentations 3:22–23, 32–33) tell us about the heart of God?

Notes:

43

God's Heart, Part Two:
Minor Prophets

Dear Kept by God,

Emotions, expressions, hopes, desires—in some way, God possesses these. At least, Scripture describes God as having these. For example, God is a jealous lover (Exodus 20:5; 34:14; Deuteronomy 4:23–24). God is nurturing (Deuteronomy 32:11; Isaiah 49:15; Luke 13:34). God also picks very specific people to deliver special messages that act out the love, concern, betrayal, and angst God experiences over us. Dramatically, God in a sense becomes vulnerable, affected by our actions.

The next section of the Bible is Part Two of the same story: God's heart for humanity. The Jewish people receive unique attention from God, both about what God wants for them and wants from them (God's blessing and their response). These next twelve books play like a broken record, repeating God's message to the Jewish people. I call it "Woos and Woes." Like a groom to his bride, God woos Israel by love. She (Israel) strays. Amidst all the other cultural options, Israel forgets God. God loves Israel too much to remain silent, and because God is *God*, he cannot allow evil to continue, especially among his people, the ones he had called out by name. Like a father to his child, God disciplines. Before he does, however, even then in love, God issues a clear warning: the woes. Woe this and woe that— are calls to wake up and pay attention. God is about to bring judgment! A woe is like saying, "Whoa! Slow down. Steer clear. Don't go down this path of death. Look! God is giving you a chance to turn from your ways, to be protected from doom." While these prophecies were historically directed to the Jewish people, by extension, the same principles of ethics and morality (and warnings for disobedience) apply to all who follow the Jewish God.

The books of the minor (as in shorter) prophets are written over the period 800–400 B.C.:

Hosea

God's love for Israel (northern kingdom of the divided Jewish kingdom) is pictured through the prophet Hosea's love for Gomer, a prostitute whom he marries.

Joel

Prophesying to Judah (southern kingdom of the divided Jewish kingdom), Joel uses a recent locust plague to illustrate the coming invasion of Babylon (which happened 605–586 B.C.) and the coming ultimate judgment, the "day of the LORD."

Amos

Prophesying to the northern kingdom, Amos, a shepherd, delivers eight warnings of judgment over the surrounding nations and Israel itself, also giving the hope of restoration.

Obadiah

Prophesying to the tribe of Judah (the descendants of Jacob), Obadiah foretells God's judgment coming to Edom (the land of the descendants of Esau, Jacob's twin brother).

Jonah

Out of his love for a godless city (Nineveh in Assyria, the most powerful kingdom in the ancient world from 886 to 625 B.C.), God sends Jonah to warn it to turn from its ways, which it does.

Micah

A prophet to Judah, Micah pronounces judgment for the people's sins (both in Israel and Judah), yet a future hope through a Messiah.

Nahum

About 150 years after Jonah, when Assyria destroyed the northern kingdom of Israel in 722 B.C., Nahum prophesies to the southern kingdom of Judah the destruction of Nineveh, the capital city of Assyria (which started in 612 B.C. when Assyria was overtaken by the new king on the block: King Nabopolassar of Babylon).

Habakkuk

Prophesying to the southern kingdom (Judah), Habakkuk asks God why Judah has not yet been judged and why God will use a wicked nation (Babylon) to punish Judah, questions that God answers.

Zephaniah

Written around 627 B.C., Zephaniah prophesies to the southern kingdom about the day of the LORD, the judgment that God will bring to the whole world, and a promise to Judah of restoration.

The last three minor prophets spoke to Jews who had already been exiled from their land.

Haggai

Prophesying to the Jews who had returned to their land after Persia conquered Babylon, Haggai instructs them around 520 B.C to rebuild the temple and announces the coming Messiah.

Zechariah

Zechariah, writing between 520–475 B.C., describes eight visions, the temple being rebuilt, the promised Messiah (Zechariah 12:10!), and encourages the exiled Jews who have returned to follow God better than their fathers and mothers did.

Malachi

Prophesying to the exiled Jewish people around 450 B.C., Malachi reminds them that their sins, not God's disinterest, have produced their trauma and pronounces the coming of both the prophet (an Elijahprototype who will announce the Messiah) and the Messiah, their blessed hope.

Several have written songs about certain books of the prophets. Check out Michael Card's "Song of Gomer," "Then They Will Know," or Andrew Peterson's "Hosea." These brilliantly illustrate those texts.

Remember that God warns us precisely to save us,

Jenny

What Do You Believe?

1. How does God feel about you? Does how God feels about you change? Why or why not?

2. Why has God not given up on the human race?

3. Will God ever give up on you (2 Timothy 2:13)?

Notes:

44

God's Forgiveness Complete: The Gospels

Dear Little Lamb of Christ,[43]

After two thousand years of conversations between God and his people came 400 years of silence. We get antsy if we don't hear from people within 24 hours. For all the laws, grace, love, and warnings God pronounces through the Old Testament, God pauses. Why? Why would God wait so long to speak again? I am not sure. What I can say is that God had already told his people everything they needed to know to follow him faithfully. They had been given enough to go on. After reading the books of seventeen prophets which repeatedly declare the sheer abandonment of God's people to God's ways, if people weren't changing their behavior, what else was there to say? I think we can trust that God was still working in the world and encouraging people, but there were no more recorded instructions to God's people for four centuries. This is the period between the Old Testament records and the New Testament writings that followed God arriving in human form (baby Jesus).

The word testament means "covenant," so the New Testament reveals God's continued plan from the Old Covenant made in the Old Testament to the new covenant God finished through God as Son, Jesus Christ. The Bible is one story of God's universal work of creation, rescue, and restoration described through these sixty-six books. Excitement, conflict, sensuality, love, trauma, drama fills these pages as God writes to us his story, the plan of history.

Four of the men, who first gave up everything to follow Jesus, ended up writing the first four books of the New Testament. You'll see significant overlap among the books since they experienced many of the same events together with Jesus. You also will see their unique temperaments, backgrounds, and personalities reflected in their writings. This variety helps to color, so to speak, the full narrative of the four books, filling in details that the other writers did not mention or emphasizing certain items in particular. These are our best records of what Jesus actually said and did.

Matthew

Matthew refers often to the kingdom of God and uses the Old Testament, specifically for the Jewish community, to demonstrate that Jesus is who he claims: the Messiah, the King God had promised them.

Mark

Writing for non-Jewish (Gentile) people, Mark describes Jesus as Christ and Son of God, the servant who suffered to save the world.

Luke

Luke, a Gentile physician, depicts Jesus as the Son of Man, giving the most details about his life and focusing on his human qualities and compassion for everyone in the world.

John

John's gospel presents Jesus as God and human, the very Word of God to the world. John's account reads differently than the other gospels. It is split into two parts, the Book of Signs (Chapters 1–12) and the Book of Glory (Chapters 13–21). Jesus fulfills many Jewish customs or "signs" to show who he is, the Light of the World.

The Greek word for gospel is literally translated "good news," so these four books are called the Gospels because they announce that the Savior of the world has arrived.

Rescued by God,

Jenny

What Do You Believe?

1. So what's the good news that Jesus brought?

2. Why do some people not follow Jesus?

3. What is this kingdom thing that Jesus mentioned? Hint: 1 Chronicles 29:11; Daniel 7:18, 27; Matthew 4:17; John 3:3–5; 18:36–37.

Notes:

45

The Church Begins: Acts

Dear Wayfarer,

You, my dear, have come so far in your faith—from not caring about God to searching for what God wants for you. It's a lifelong journey, a pilgrimage. So many stories and verses in the Bible speak of this pilgrimage (such as Psalm 84:5–12). *Acts* describes especially well the pilgrimage for the Jewish people, for those who recognized that Jesus was God's Chosen One. Can you imagine the disorientation they might have had? How would they relate to God now that the Promised One had come? His final sacrifice ended all need for further animal sacrifice. Their sins had been paid for and forgiven. His death ripped open the Jewish temple veil that hid (or rather, protected) them from God's glory. Now, God himself stood in the gap. How would believers relate to this one true God *(YHWH)* who had deleted the distance between them?

They had no idea.

So they waited.

And prayed.

And waited.

Then something happened.

God answered.

Actually, God had previously told them what was going to happen through the prophet Joel (Joel 2:28–32), but so much of prophecy is only understood in hindsight. Read what Peter explains in Acts 2:14–33. God the Spirit had only been upon people in spurts in the Old Testament. Whereas the presence of God previously was housed in a literal temple building, God the Spirit now could rest upon God's people with permanence. The temple of God had been a physical structure, but because of the final sacrifice for sin (God the Son), the temple could now be the human body.

Acts marks this seismic shift as well as another: the beginning of the church. Matthew interestingly mentions this word in his gospel book (Matthew 16:18). *Acts*, written by Luke as the sequel to the gospel of Luke, relays the history of those who believed in the gospel message after Jesus rose from the dead and describes how the church functioned and grew and spread, largely by persecution as you will read.

Pentecost originally was the Jewish festival of the Feast of Weeks that occurs fifty days after Passover (Leviticus 23:15–16; Deuteronomy 16:9). After the Messiah's resurrection, during this feast, the Spirit of God descended upon believers. Pentecost for Christians refers to the Spirit's coming upon God's people and the beginning of the church (Acts 1:4–5, 8; 2:38).

By the Spirit,

Jenny

What Do You Believe?

1. Since Pentecost, when does the Spirit of God enter a Christian?

2. Is it important for Christians to be a part of a local church? Why or why not?

3. Who are you now (Acts 1:8)?

Notes:

46

Living like a Christian, Part One: Paul's Letters

Dear Temple of God's Spirit,

Good morning! I do pray that this letter finds you well and content, if not satisfied. As you know, God showers us with so many gifts in this life, and we still thirst for more. As it should be! We were made for much more than this present shattered reality. It is a good thing to hunger, to open yourself up to God to fill you, to want more. Desire was created by God to be filled. That also means waiting, sometimes a very long time (to us). Take heart; God will not cheat you. In the meantime, live out goodness, live purely. Paul's letters provide great counsel. He wrote thirteen letters to various churches or church leaders throughout the Middle East and Asia Minor. The titles may be foreign to us now, but most are named for the city or region in which the church was located.

Perhaps you can think of these letters as what a father would say to instruct his daughter, for Paul held a compassionate love for these people starting out in their faith and a fatherly concern for their discipline when needed. He stressed the basics of what a new life in Christ means. It means turning from your old way of life, who you thought you were, to find God and let God re-form you. First century Rome was a hedonistic (absorbed with self-pleasure, especially sexual) culture as is our 21st century. Paul stepped into the middle of their lives and explained how one who follows Christ should live—very differently! You'll recognize in Paul's writing the themes that I described earlier: loyalty, goodness, innocence, suffering, service, etc.

Here are his books in one sentence:

Romans

Paul declares to the church in Rome that God alone saves; reaching God is by faith through Jesus Christ, not social standing, ethnic background, or any human status or effort.

First Corinthians

Paul instructs the church in Corinth that following Christ is a radical change of thought and behavior, both personally and as a group.

Second Corinthians

Paul writes to the church in Corinth of his travel itinerary, his leadership, and further instructions on how to live like a Christian.

Galatians

Paul writes to the church in Galatia about law and grace and the freedom that comes in living by God's Spirit.

Ephesians

In a letter to the church in Ephesus, Paul describes what God has done for each believer, their identity in Christ, and what their responsibilities are.

Philippians

In a letter to the church in Philippi about the life of Jesus, Paul depicts how suffering, humility, confidence, and peace relate to each believer in how they live.

Colossians

Paul reminds the church in Colossae that Christ is over everything in every way, and the freedom he offers is for a new way of living.

First Thessalonians

Emphasizing that Christ will return to earth, Paul writes to the church in Thessalonica to persevere and stay true to God rather than imitate the surrounding culture.

Second Thessalonians

In a second letter to the church in Thessalonica, Paul describes what the "day of the Lord" means to encourage them in their present suffering to keep living faithfully to God.

First Timothy

Paul writes to his disciple, Timothy, in charge of the Christian work in Ephesus and Asia Minor, on church conduct and leadership.

Second Timothy

In Paul's second letter, he describes the character and behavior that Timothy should show.

Titus

Paul addresses Titus, a leader to the churches of Crete, about how to set up the churches, what to require of leaders, emphasizing that what Scripture says actually matters and that genuine faith leads to action.

Philemon

Paul writes to Philemon, a church leader in Colossae, about how he should relate to his slave, Onesimus, as a brother in a time when slavery was prevalent in Roman society, relaying larger lessons on forgiveness, love, and relationships.

Paul covers much ground and what he says for us to do is this: Love God (that is, do what God says), love your neighbor and enemy, and hate evil.

I hope you love the Scripture as much as I have and more. It is a treasure few seek, but those who do become rich. Being rich, of course, is not just the amount in one's bank account. I'm talking about being rich in wisdom, rich in love, rich in peace. Money may come, and Paul talks about the pros and cons of that too along the way in these letters.

Godspeed, which is to say, may you remain in the will of God on your way,

Jenny

What Do You Believe?

1. Take a few weeks to read these books. What stands out to you?

2. What differences or similarities do you find between their first-century, Mediterranean and Middle Eastern cultures (the 1st century Mediterranean and Middle East) and ours?

3. What does grace mean, specifically, God's grace to us?

4. After reading these books, what areas of your life were you personally challenged to change?

Notes:

47

Living like a Christian, Part Two: Other Apostles' Letters

Dear Valued,

The next set of eight letters are grouped because they are written by other apostles, those who actually knew Jesus. We're not quite certain who wrote *Hebrews*, but James, Peter, John, and Jude, possibly the brother of Jesus,[44] wrote the letters that bear their names. John, of the first twelve, the only of Jesus's original disciples not to abandon him at his hour of death, wrote *Revelation*, which I've saved for my next letter.

Here are my one sentence summaries:

Hebrews

> Hebrews presents Jesus the Christ as better than all the prophets, angels, and Moses and as the high priest in whom to place faith, masterfully tying the Old and New Testaments together.

James

> James, the oldest younger brother of Jesus, addresses descendants of the twelve Jewish tribes, emphasizing how people of true faith act, for example, when tested, tempted, and speaking.

First Peter

Peter writes to believers throughout the region about how to live unstained lives, in submission and even suffering, by the grace of God.

Second Peter

Peter's second letter summarizes the confidence that believers have in the Christian message and warns that some will try to change its meaning.

First John

In his first letter, John emphasizes the shift in life-style that a believer makes and that loving God means doing what God has said to do.

Second John

Despite those who say otherwise, John repeats in this second letter: love means obeying what God has said to do.

Third John

John writes to Gaius, applauding his loyalty to truth and his hospitality toward Christians, and encourages him to be good.

Jude

> Jude describes how to recognize and deal with lying leaders in the church and what those faithful to Christ should do.

I am nearly finished reviewing, very briefly, the written words that God inspired. I have given you a mere morsel, like a tiny chocolate chip, compared to what the Bible has for you. These sixty-six books can be read and reread, and never will you reach the end of their insight. I promise. You will continue to change and grow and have new hurdles, so keep reading it. Certain things will stand out to you in the future that had not before; you will forget what you read; you will learn more about yourself and realize how certain verses then relate; your love will grow in knowledge and depth of understanding, for surely that is my prayer for you (Philippians 1:9). The thing about seeking God is that you just have to show up and ask God honestly for help. He is merciful to do the rest.

Affectionately,

Jenny

What Do You Believe?

1.   What is so important about this thing called faith? Hint: Hebrews 11.

2.   Why does living like a Christian include suffering?

3.   What is the current cultural definition of love?

4.   What is God's definition? Hint: John 15:13; Romans 5:8.

Notes:

48

Heaven is for Real and not full of Marshmallow-Cheeked Angels: Revelation

Dear Crowned,

Actually, heaven won't be the only thing for real. When Jesus Christ returns to this earth and renews this broken world, a new heaven and a new earth will exist. You will not be an angel; we will not be floating on pillowy clouds. Those who have died are held temporarily in heaven, not to stay there (Colossians 3:1–4; 1 Thessalonians 4:14–17; Revelation 21:1–3). Christ's return to earth will start this raising of believers from the dead. To do what? We will live on the new earth in a similar way to what we experience now, although changed. We will hike mountains, dance, oversee projects, laugh at hilarious jokes, and some will have special positions of leadership (Matthew 19:28; Revelation 4:4). What we do in this life matters for the next (2 Corinthians 5:10; Revelation 22:12).

Here are a few notes about the last book God gave to us:

1. The book's title is *Revelation*. The word is singular, not plural. John, who writes the book, receives *one* revelation—the revelation of Jesus Christ. John describes what he sees in a vision.

People interpret his message differently, mostly about what timeline he is discussing and what the symbols represent.

2. Jesus, the actual person, will return to our world, starting the new life we will enjoy.
3. The book completes God's story, but do not think this the end. To quote my friend Megan, "Good stories never end." God's story has three parts: creation, rescue, and renewal (of the heavens and earth).

Revelation makes this point: Jesus ushered in a new reality (the kingdom) at his death and resurrection. The book is the completion of God's grand story of creation, salvation, and restoration. Life, heaven, and earth, will be recreated. The polluted oceans. Animal predators. Our failing memories. Our decaying bodies. Our hearts. Those who have believed God and all of creation will be made new.

Christians have interpreted this book differently in basically one of three ways. People differ on what the characters represent (the woman, the beast, the dragon) and how Christ's reign of 1000 years on the earth occurs (Revelation 20). Is the period of 1000 years to be taken literally or metaphorically? The main views are amillennialism, premillennialism, and postmillennalism— huge words to discuss with your discipler. The revelation, though, is this: Jesus Christ is coming back to rescue us and make all things right!

Looking forward to forever with you,

Jenny

What Do You Believe?

1. Why would Jesus need to return to this world? Hint: Isaiah 9:7; 1 Corinthians 6:9–11; James 2:5.

2. What kinds of activities would you like to do on the new earth?

3. What do you think you will like most about being with God?

Notes:

Special Topics

49

Weekly Questions

Dear Friend of God,

Here is a smattering of my favorite questions to ask of the person you are discipling, to be asked by the one discipling you, or within an intimate small group. Often. I'd say weekly. How is your heart doing?

Love,

Jenny

Questions

1. What do you desire more than anything else?
2. What consumes your thoughts?
3. What fears threaten you?[45]
4. Has how you have spoken to your spouse or family member shown that your heart is content with what God is for you in Christ?[46]
5. What sins have you committed?
6. Who do you need to forgive?
7. From whom do you need to ask forgiveness?
8. How have you spent money this week? Did it point people to God?
9. What do I need to give to God?
10. What is tempting me?

John Wesley, a preacher in the 1700s, offered these questions among others:[47]

1. Did I give God time to speak to me through the Bible today?
2. When did I last speak to someone about my faith?
3. How do I spend my spare time?
4. Am I a slave to dress, friends, work, or habits?
5. Am I enjoying prayer?

50

Lies You Have Been Taught

Lie: You can have everything.

Truth: Just like the song says, "you can't always get what you want" in life. Sometimes you'll get things that you definitely don't want.

Lie: You are perfect just the way you are.

Truth: Almost. You are beautiful and broken and need to be made new.

Lie: You are worthless.

Truth: Rubbish! You are priceless.

Lie: Love must be earned.

Truth: God's love is given freely, without cost to us. God loves you so much that he did everything to save you.

Lie: You can be anything you want to be.

Truth: You can be some things you want to be. That doesn't mean you shouldn't try.

Lie: Forgiving means forgetting.

Truth: Forgiving is not enabling.

Lie: You are weak if you cry.

Truth: God wept (John 11:35). So there must be more to it; something about crying is good.

Lie: No one will find out.

Truth: Uhmmm. One of the scariest verses in the Bible to me is: "For God will bring every deed into judgment, including every hidden thing, whether it is good or evil" (Ecclesiastes 12:14). See also Matthew 12:36 and 1 Corinthians 3:13.

Lie: God won't give you more than you can handle.

Truth: False. God wants you to recognize that you can't handle it. God won't give you more than he can handle.

Lie: I will be happy once I am married.

Truth: Being single or married does not make you more or less of a valuable person. Even if you desire something else, enjoy what you have now.

Lie: Hide your shame and guilt.

Truth: Nope, wrong again. Bring your dark secrets into the Light to be pierced and healed by Love. You can be forgiven.

Lie: God wants me to be happy.

Truth: Ultimately, I guess, but not by what that word means when most people use it. God wants us to be good.

Lie: I am alone.

Truth: You are never, not once, alone on this earth (Psalm 139:8; Proverbs 18:24).

Finding the Right Guy and Shacking Up

Dear Hopeful,

Don't look back. Don't slow down. Keep running your race for God. Turning around or looking behind slows you down and gets you off rhythm. Keep running toward God. One day, if the right guy comes along, you'll see him in your peripheral vision, running alongside of you, running in the same direction—toward God. One day you'll look up and see someone with at least as quick a pace as you, running toward God. He might even be a bit in front of you. You won't have to slow down, stop, turn, or settle for the man that God wants for you. Keep on running. You have others by your side in the meantime.

As you know, it's commonplace in our day to live with members of the opposite sex and/or live with your sexual partner before marriage. Why might that not be a good idea? Because Christians hold to the virtues of holiness and purity. The world in its wisdom will act in many ways that we, as Christians, will not participate.

Within the U.S., cohabitation exploded in occurrence with the 1960s revolution of thinking. Liberation became doing whatever you felt like doing. A pattern of thinking then emerged from the children of the 1980s and 1990s whose parents had failed miserably at marriage: cohabitation is pragmatic, almost required, to try things out in a desperate attempt to avoid the divorce of their parents. The very couples from the 1960s and 1970s—who were supposedly the first generation to find sexual freedom—found marriage more difficult. Why? Because commitment requires constraint. When you haven't been practicing good boundaries before marriage, why would you suddenly have them in marriage? Many cohabiting couples break up before marriage, as you know, and research has shown that for those who married *after* living together, their marriages had a higher rate of divorce or separation than marriages without premarital cohabitation.[48]

This supports God's intentional plan in the first place, to protect us, to give us a hope and a future, and a solid relationship for building a family. God's design is that we not engage in the most intimate of activities with another soul before we make a formal commitment to God and the public to remain with them the rest of our lives.

Everybody talks about doing your own thing and being unconventional. So why not be odd and prepare for marriage in the way that God has commanded? The type of man or woman who is willing to show sexual restraint *before* marriage will more likely be loyal *in* marriage. I'm not saying that two who mistakenly lived together first won't ever work out, but they miss out on the greater good that could have been theirs by not living together first. It's an issue of repentance and holiness; it boils down to whether or not you take God at God's Word enough to live it out.

You are loved,

Jenny

Are All Religions the Same?

Dear Christ-follower,

I was in my doctor's office one day, and the resident physician brought up the subject of religion while inspecting my knee. He stated that, having attended an Episcopal high school and though not a Christian himself but engaged to a Catholic, he considered that all religions taught the same thing: be a good person, follow the Golden Rule, etc.

What if all religions are basically the same? What if that is true? I began to think of other questions that would raise:

Why then did Christ die? The cruelty of an innocent man being killed for no purpose would call into question the validity (that is, goodness) of that religious system, meaning Christianity.

What is good? Religions differ in their definition.

With each religion evaluating behavior differently by different judgment systems, how are innocence and injustice determined? If there is no judgment, can there be justice? How are victims repaid?

So, whatever religion we do or do not follow, I submit that it is not because they are all the same. Why do we believe what we do?

What if that belief—that all religions are similar and equally valid—is a lie? All other world religions describe a system of humanity striving toward and reaching out to please a supernatural power(s). This is the similarity among the religious systems of performance-based acceptance in trying to "be a good person" and satisfy the god(s). One religion, however, flips that. Christianity describes a system of one Deity reaching down to grasp humanity in their utter helplessness. Humanity earned judgment and death by their deeds; the Christian hope is redemption, being given a substitute (Jesus Christ) who paid our debt in death to rescue us and literally was raised from the dead (another uniqueness among religions). If our end is judgment, the question to us then will not be "Were you a good person?," but "Did you believe that I (Jesus) loved you?"[49] Do you believe that Jesus had to die for you? Why? See John 3:16; 14:6.

Keep asking good questions,

Jenny

Why Do Bad Things Happen to Good People?

Dear Earnest,

It's important in answering this question to consider what explanations other religions offer. How would atheists respond? Is our heartache in life random and a process of natural selection? Is our suffering a result of our desires, according to Buddhism?

According to Christianity, no one is good (Psalms 14:1–3; 53:1–3; Ecclesiastes 7:20; Romans 3:10–12, 23). Second of all, perhaps we're asking the wrong question altogether. Why don't we ever ask the opposite question:

Why do good things happen to bad people?

This may be the harder question to answer. People from other religions address why evil and suffering pervade the world, but do they explain this: how does good exist? From where did it come? Who are we? Why do we deserve good necessarily? But back to the original question.

Why do bad things happen to good people? Perhaps another question to ask is, "Why do people experience pain, suffering, grief, death, and injustice?" The Christian God answers this through the whole of Scripture. Part of the answer is this: we—*we*—rebelled against God's order. Against God. I get stuck on imagining our audacity to do such a thing, and each of us still do it every single day (James 1:13–15; 3:14–16). For example, some choice comes to you, whether to lie on this application, or with-hold something from someone illegitimately, or to entertain a certain thought. Someone or something prompts us to stop and reconsider. Then we proceed to in-tentionally do what we know is wrong. That is how bad things happen . . . to bad people.

Another part of the answer is this: some angels re-belled against God's order, chief among them, Satan (Revelation 12:7–13). So other spiritual forces of evil are lurking to lure us into traps that we willingly and/or un-wittingly walk (Ephesians 6:10–17). Rebellion has caused a chaotic, cosmic war here, fantastic and incredible. God, in fact, went to great lengths to give us an answer, even if we do not grasp it fully.

Go to YouTube, look up "Ravi Zacharias," and watch a couple of his clips.[50] Ravi Zacharias grew up in India, con-verted to Christianity, and immigrated to Canada and the U.S. He shares compelling explanations to this question. Nabeel Qureshi, who converted from Islam, also describes his first story of suffering.[51]

Remember, only God is intrinsically good (Mark 10:18; Luke 18:19).

Filled with hope,

Jenny

Conclusion

Dear Reader,

I write these things to you so that you may *live* (1 John 2:1). This is my last letter, for now. I didn't cover everything, clearly, but walking with Christ is a lifelong trail. Like learning to practice forgiveness or how to share your faith, you will need to learn other important virtues and practices to faithfully live as a Christian. I leave you in the care of your discipler and your local church. You will have help along the way as different needs in your life arise; others will join your journey and enrich your life. How wonderful it has been to walk with you this far. This is my first summary of what loving God involves (1 John 1:5–7). Love well!

God is for you (Romans 5:8). God is with you always, everywhere. Now go and be who God says you are in Christ (John 1:12–13; 1 John 3:1–3), which is to say, go and do what God has said (Matthew 28:19–20).

With love in Christ,

Jenny

Further Reading

Here are my suggestions for further study. This is a woefully incomplete list, but it will get you started.

Understanding Christian Beliefs

Mere Christianity, C. S. Lewis
Jesus among Secular Gods: The Countercultural Claims of Christ, Ravi Zacharias

Why the Bible is Authentic

Jesus Revisited, Daniel Wallace
Google "Daniel Wallace Jesus Video." His YouTube videos on the subject are brilliant.

Confession

Confessions, Augustine (354–430), Bishop of Hippo Regius (what is now Annaba, Algeria), translated by Sarah Rudens. This is one of our church father's realization of the sin in his life.

Culture and Calling

Culture Care: Reconnecting with Beauty for our Common Life, Makoto Fujimura

Evangelism: Sharing your Faith

Evangelism Explosion, D. James Kennedy

Generosity and Joy

Free of Charge, Miroslav Volf
Enjoy: Finding the Freedom to Delight Daily in God's Good Gifts, Trillia Newbell

God's Spirit

The Promise, Tony Evans
Embraced by the Spirit, Chuck Swindoll

Intimacy

Boundaries, Henry Cloud and John Townsend
Spiritual Friendship, Wesley Hill

Marriage

The Meaning of Marriage, Timothy and Kathy Keller
Love and War, John and Staci Eldredge

Money

Raising Money-Smart Kids, Judy and Ron Blue
Financial Peace University, DVD guide, Dave Ramsey
Naked and Unashamed: 10 Money Conversations Every Couple Must Have, Ericka Young

Prayer

Most anything written by E. M. Bounds

Fervent: A Woman's Battle Plan to Serious, Specific and Strategic Prayer, Priscilla Shirer

Sexuality

Soul Virgins: Redefining Single Sexuality, Doug Rosenau
Redeeming Sex: Naked Conversations about Sexuality and Spirituality, Debra Hirsch
Not Marked: Finding Hope and Healing after Sexual Abuse, Mary DeMuth

Suffering

When God Weeps, Joni Eareckson Tada and Steven Estes
Where is God When It Hurts?, Philip Yancey
Blindsided by God: Disappointment, Suffering, and the Untamable Goodness of God, Peter Chin

Understanding Christian Practices

Celebration of Discipline: The Path to Spiritual Growth, Richard Foster
The Spirit of the Disciplines: Understanding How God Changes Lives, Dallas Willard
Sacred Pauses: Spiritual Practices for Personal Renewal, April Yamasaki

Studying God's Word

Living by the Book, Howard Hendricks

Nelson's Quick Reference Bible Handbook (gives an overview of the Bible)

Women of the Word, Jen Wilkin

How to Study Your Bible, Kay Arthur

About the Author

Jenny McGill (PhD, King's College London) serves as a dean at Indiana Wesleyan University and an adjunct faculty member at Dallas Theological Seminary, having worked in international education and intercultural consulting with clients and students from over sixty nations.

A pastor's wife, she has experienced ministry overseas, in a megachurch, a church plant, and now middle America. Connect with her at www.jennymcgill.com and @drjennymcgill.

About Gospel-Centered Discipleship

You may have noticed that there are a lot of resources available for theological education, church planting, and missional church, but not for discipleship. We noticed too, so we started Gospel-Centered Discipleship to address the need for reliable resources on a whole range of discipleship issues.

When we use the term "gospel-centered," we aren't trying to divide Christians into camps, but to promote a way of following Jesus that is centered on the gospel of grace. While all disciples of Jesus believe the gospel is central to Christianity, we often live as if religious rules or spiritual license actually form the center of discipleship.

Jesus calls us to displace those things and replace them with the gospel. We're meant to apply the benefits of the gospel to our lives every day, not to merely bank on them for a single instance of "being saved." A gospel-centered disciple returns to the gospel over and over again, to receive, apply, and spread God's forgiveness and grace into every aspect of life.

Gospel-Centered Discipleship
Resources

Visit GCDiscipleship.com/Books.

The Christian life is knowing God. It is not an impersonal knowledge of bare facts but one rooted in wonder at "the light of the knowledge of the glory of God in the face of Jesus Christ" (2 Cor. 4:6). It is knowing that basks in the glories of the gospel.

In *Gospel Glories from A to Z*, Kelly Havrilla works to reflect some of that glory onto each page as she connects deep biblical truths through the structure of the alphabet. Useful for both those new to the beauty of Christianity and those looking for a fresh way to grow deeper this book aims to make God's grace abundantly clear and accessible. Our hope is that this reflection will spark a desire to venture into deeper waves of gospel glories.

As the Protestant church celebrates the 500th anniversary of the Reformation the question of the authority and power of the Word of God for everyday life is still raised by many. Through this collection of essays, the Gospel-Centered Discipleship team seeks to demonstrate not only the rich theological implications of the authority of the Bible, but also the life-altering power of God's Word for everyday, ordinary life.

GCD's aim is to see the Word of God "make, mature, and multiply disciples of Jesus." As Martin Luther declared, "the Bible is alive, it speaks to me, it has feet, it runs after me, it has hands, it lays hold [of] me." He was announcing the power of the Bible "above all earthly powers."

After fifteen plus years of vocational ministry, Ben Connelly had an epiphany. He had missed the great commission. He was really good at keeping Christians happy and really bad at making disciples. *A Pastor's Guide to Everyday Mission* helps those in paid ministry positions rediscover—and live—their life as God's missionaries, even as they minister to God's people.

We stand in the already and not yet. We are disciples serving between Christ's coming and his coming again. As we look backward, we see an astonishing baby boy cradled in his mother's arms and the saving life he will lead. Looking forward, we see a complete kingdom and restoration of all things. We celebrate Christmas only after grappling with the hope fulfilled and the hope still waiting.

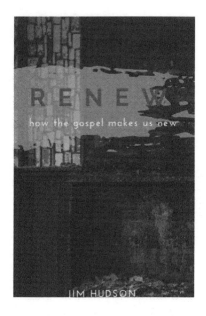

Too often we limit the power of the gospel to its blessings for us in the afterlife. We fail to see how the power of God, which raised Jesus from the dead, fuels our day-to-day battle against sin in this life. *Renew* shows us the grace of God is able to change us now.

For those looking to break specific sinful habits and temptations as well as those looking to gain a better grasp of how a Christian grows *Renew* speaks to the power of the gospel today.

End Notes

¹ I, by no means, am the first to write about discipleship. Apart from sections of the Bible, the *Epistle to Diognetus*, circa 2nd century, is perhaps the earliest surviving manuscript of a discipleship manual. See https://en.wikipedia.org/wiki/Epistle_to_Diognetus.

² For example, https://youtu.be/-aKpEGHZdGs.

³ Adapted from Staci Eldredge, *Becoming Myself*, p. 247 and John and Staci Eldredge, *Love and War*, p. 212.

⁴ The exact date of the origin for the Apostles' Creed is unknown. The earliest evidence is in a letter to the Council of Milan in 390. See http://www.christianitytoday.com/biblestudies/articles/churchhomeleadership/nicene-apostles-creeds.html.

⁵ Catholic when capitalized refers to the Roman Catholic Church. When not capitalized, catholic means the wider, global body of Christ, the church, comprised of all Christians, whatever the denomination.

⁶ The Nicene Creed was officially adopted by Council of Chalcedon in 451, although its origin dates from the Council of Nicea in 325.

⁷ This marked phrase is debated among Christians.

⁸ We cannot know really if another person is a Christian or not, other than what they tell us and how they live. But there are reasonable signs for the person to make their own self-assessment. Jesus compares people to fruit trees and what kind of fruit they bear in Matthew 7:15-20; Luke 6:43–46; 13:6–9.

⁹ The video on the Trinity is available at https://youtu.be/KQLf-gaUoQCw.

¹⁰ This video is available at http://csntm.org/Resources/DVD.

¹¹ See https://bible.org/seriespage/7-bible-holy-canon-scripture.

¹² Our calendar actually changed to mark the coming of God's chosen One to save the world. From B.C. (before Christ) to A.D. (*anno Domini*, Latin for "in the year of our Lord"). Interestingly, the notation has changed to

B.C.E. (before the common era) and C.E. (common era) and marks the same event.

[13] For a detailed description, see Jenny McGill, *Religious Identity and Cultural Negotiation*, Pickwick, 2016, p. 213–14.

[14] See Acts 9:2.

[15] The Puritans failed miserably in not calling out the inhumane treatment of slaves. Christians in each generation nail some things well and utterly fail in other respects.

[16] Adapted from *The Valley of Vision: A Collection of Puritan Prayers and Devotions*, edited by Arthur Bennett, Banner of Truth Trust, 1975, p. xv.

[17] Pastor Kevin McGill explains this well in his sermon on 26 July 2015 in which he uses the illustration of the mayor gorging himself on chocolate in the movie, *Chocolat* (www.cornerstonenwi.com).

[18] McGill, *Religious Identity and Cultural Negotiation*, p. 208–09.

[19] Matthew 13:45–46.

[20] Side note: This verse doesn't say that you *won't* have trouble if you fear God, but that it won't have to touch you. You are so at peace in fearing God, trouble won't have to disturb you.

[21] Mitali Perkins, "When God Writes Your Life Story" *Christianity Today* Jan-Feb 2016, p. 96–97.

[22] Dietrich Bonhoeffer in Eric Metaxas, *Bonhoeffer: Pastor, Martyr, Prophet, Spy*, Thomas Nelson, 2010, p. 384.

[23] Quoted from an interview by Sarah Nielsen in *Just Between Us*, Fall 2015.

[24] Romans 9:8; Galatians 4:28.

[25] Kevin McGill, sermon, Cornerstone Community Church, July 26, 2015.

[26] I use heart, mind, soul, and spirit interchangeably.

[27] Ephesians 5:11.

[28] Richard Foster, *Celebration of Discipline*, HarperOne, 1998 p. 90–95.

[29] Emphasis added. C. John Collins, "Abiding in the Vine," *Christianity Today*, March 2016, p. 49.

[30] Levi Lusko, *Through the Eyes of a Lion*, W Publishing Group, 2015, p. 104.

[31] Woody Glenn, Skillman Bible Church sermon, "Changing our Perspective on Money," March 16, 2014 available on iTunes at www.google.com/search?q=skillman+Bible+church+sermons&ie=UTF-8&oe=UTF-8&hl=en-us&client-safari.

[32] We serve from our position as sons and daughters of God (Galatians 4:7).

[33] See her post at http://gcdiscipleship.com/2016/03/17/how-we-read-the-bible-matters, accessed 20 June 2016.

[34] See http://www.markeckart.com/questions.html.

[35] Donald Whitney, *Spiritual Disciplines for the Christian Life*, NavPress, 1991, p. 60.

[36] Excerpt from Sandra Glahn's 2/3/15 blog post, www.blogs.bible.org/engage/sandra_glahn/jesus_calling.

[37] Alex Kocman wrote an excellent Facebook post on this very issue available at https://m.facebook.com/story.php?story_fbid=10212137699091857&id=1057171494.

[38] Abraham lived around 2000 B.C.; David lived around 1000 B.C.

[39] God made covenants with Adam, Abraham, Noah, Moses, and David (Genesis 1:26-30; 2:16–17; 9:11; Deuteronomy 11; 2 Samuel 7:8–16). The last and final covenant is the new covenant made by God Himself in Jesus to meet the terms of the covenant that humanity had not (Matthew 26:28; Hebrews 9:15).

[40] My favorite summary so far is http://www.dts.edu/the-table/play/genocide-old-testament. Additional thoughtful responses to the charge of genocide and the continuity of the same God between Testaments include those by Justin Taylor (https://www.thegospelcoalition.org/blogs/justin-taylor/how-could-god-command-genocide-in-the-old-testament-2), J.D. Greear (https://jdgreear.com/blog/does-the-old-testament-advocate-genocide), and Mark Buchanan (https://www.christianitytoday.com/ct/2013/july-august/can-we-trust-god-of-genocide.html), respectively.

[41] The poetry of the Bible include these books listed as well as Lamentations and the psalms listed in other books such as in Exodus, 1 Samuel, etc.

[42] Dr. Constable's study notes are available at http://soniclight.com/constable/notes.htm.

[43] John 10:4–5.

[44] If the James of Jude 1:1 is the same James mentioned in Galatians 1:19, then this would be true.

[45] Questions 1–3 are adapted from Jonathan Dodson, *Gospel-Centered Discipleship*, p. 155–56.

[46] This question is adapted from those posed by Sam Storms in *A Sincere and Pure Devotion to Christ*, cited in Helen Kim's dissertation,

End Notes

1. I, by no means, am the first to write about discipleship. Apart from sections of the Bible, the *Epistle to Diognetus*, circa 2nd century, is perhaps the earliest surviving manuscript of a discipleship manual. See https://en.wikipedia.org/wiki/Epistle_to_Diognetus.

2. For example, https://youtu.be/-aKpEGHZdGs.

3. Adapted from Staci Eldredge, *Becoming Myself*, p. 247 and John and Staci Eldredge, *Love and War*, p. 212.

4. The exact date of the origin for the Apostles' Creed is unknown. The earliest evidence is in a letter to the Council of Milan in 390. See http://www.christianitytoday.com/biblestudies/articles/churchhomeleadership/nicene-apostles-creeds.html.

5. Catholic when capitalized refers to the Roman Catholic Church. When not capitalized, catholic means the wider, global body of Christ, the church, comprised of all Christians, whatever the denomination.

6. The Nicene Creed was officially adopted by Council of Chalcedon in 451, although its origin dates from the Council of Nicea in 325.

7. This marked phrase is debated among Christians.

8. We cannot know really if another person is a Christian or not, other than what they tell us and how they live. But there are reasonable signs for the person to make their own self-assessment. Jesus compares people to fruit trees and what kind of fruit they bear in Matthew 7:15-20; Luke 6:43–46; 13:6–9.

9. The video on the Trinity is available at https://youtu.be/KQLf-gaUoQCw.

10. This video is available at http://csntm.org/Resources/DVD.

11. See https://bible.org/seriespage/7-bible-holy-canon-scripture.

12. Our calendar actually changed to mark the coming of God's cho-
    sen One to save the world. From B.C. (before Christ) to A.D. (*anno
    Domini*, Latin for "in the year of our Lord"). Interestingly, the no-
    tation has changed to B.C.E. (before the common era) and C.E.
    (common era) and marks the same event.

13. For a detailed description, see Jenny McGill, *Religious Identity and
    Cultural Negotiation*, Pickwick, 2016, p. 213–14.

14. See Acts 9:2.

15. The Puritans failed miserably in not calling out the inhumane
    treatment of slaves. Christians in each generation nail some
    things well and utterly fail in other respects.

16. Adapted from *The Valley of Vision: A Collection of Puritan Prayers
    and Devotions*, edited by Arthur Bennett, Banner of Truth Trust,
    1975, p. xv.

17. Pastor Kevin McGill explains this well in his sermon on 26 July
    2015 in which he uses the illustration of the mayor gorging him-
    self on chocolate in the movie, *Chocolat*
    (www.cornerstonenwi.com).

18. McGill, *Religious Identity and Cultural Negotiation*, p. 208–09.

19. Matthew 13:45–46.

20. Side note: This verse doesn't say that you *won't* have trouble if
    you fear God, but that it won't have to touch you. You are so at
    peace in fearing God, trouble won't have to disturb you.

21. Mitali Perkins, "When God Writes Your Life Story" *Christianity
    Today* Jan-Feb 2016, p. 96–97.

22. Dietrich Bonhoeffer in Eric Metaxas, *Bonhoeffer: Pastor, Martyr,
    Prophet, Spy*, Thomas Nelson, 2010, p. 384.

23. Quoted from an interview by Sarah Nielsen in *Just Between Us*,
    Fall 2015.

24. Romans 9:8; Galatians 4:28.

25. Kevin McGill, sermon, Cornerstone Community Church, July 26,
    2015.

26. I use heart, mind, soul, and spirit interchangeably.

27. Ephesians 5:11.

28. Richard Foster, *Celebration of Discipline,* HarperOne, 1998 p. 90–95.

29. Emphasis added. C. John Collins, "Abiding in the Vine," *Christianity Today*, March 2016, p. 49.

30. Levi Lusko, *Through the Eyes of a Lion*, W Publishing Group, 2015, p. 104.

31. Woody Glenn, Skillman Bible Church sermon, "Changing our Perspective on Money," March 16, 2014 available on iTunes at www.google.com/search?q=skillman+Bible+church+sermons&ie=UTF-8&oe=UTF-8&hl=en-us&client-safari.

32. We serve from our position as sons and daughters of God (Galatians 4:7).

33. See her post at http://gcdiscipleship.com/2016/03/17/how-we-read-the-bible-matters, accessed 20 June 2016.

34. See http://www.markeckart.com/questions.html.

35. Donald Whitney, *Spiritual Disciplines for the Christian Life*, NavPress, 1991, p. 60.

36. Excerpt from Sandra Glahn's 2/3/15 blog post, www.blogs.bible.org/engage/sandra_glahn/jesus_calling.

37. Alex Kocman wrote an excellent Facebook post on this very issue available at https://m.facebook.com/story.php?story_fbid=10212137699091857&id=1057171494.

38. Abraham lived around 2000 B.C.; David lived around 1000 B.C.

39. God made covenants with Adam, Abraham, Noah, Moses, and David (Genesis 1:26-30; 2:16–17; 9:11; Deuteronomy 11; 2 Samuel 7:8–16). The last and final covenant is the new covenant made by God Himself in Jesus to meet the terms of the covenant that humanity had not (Matthew 26:28; Hebrews 9:15).

40. My favorite summary so far is http://www.dts.edu/the-table/play/genocide-old-testament. Additional thoughtful responses to the charge of genocide and the continuity of the

same God between Testaments include those by Justin Taylor (https://www.thegospelcoalition.org/blogs/justin-taylor/how-could-god-command-genocide-in-the-old-testament-2), J.D. Greear (https://jdgreear.com/blog/does-the-old-testament-advocate-genocide), and Mark Buchanan (https://www.christianitytoday.com/ct/2013/july-august/can-we-trust-god-of-genocide.html), respectively.

41. The poetry of the Bible include these books listed as well as Lamentations and the psalms listed in other books such as in Exodus, 1 Samuel, etc.

42. Dr. Constable's study notes are available at http://soniclight.com/constable/notes.htm.

43. John 10:4–5.

44. If the James of Jude 1:1 is the same James mentioned in Galatians 1:19, then this would be true.

45. Questions 1–3 are adapted from Jonathan Dodson, *Gospel-Centered Discipleship*, p. 155–56.

46. This question is adapted from those posed by Sam Storms in *A Sincere and Pure Devotion to Christ*, cited in Helen Kim's dissertation, "Developing a Discipleship Culture in the Church through Increased "with-God" Conversations." Assemblies of God Theological Seminary, 2015.

47. Adapted from Helen Kim, "Developing a Discipleship Culture in the Church," p. 160.

48. Bruce Wydick, "Why Married Sex is Social Justice," *Christianity Today*, July/August 2016, p. 74–75.

49. Brennan Manning poses this second question. See https://youtu.be/pQi_IDV2bgM.

50. For example, https://www.youtube.com/watch?v=it7mhQ8fEq0.

51. See https://www.youtube.com/watch?v=psrvQZj68h4.

Made in the USA
Middletown, DE
05 September 2018